SONGS

OF THE

INNER LIFE

For additional information, contact:

Sage's Play

P.O. Box 484

Ashland, Oregon 97520

Cover design: Robert Frost Design

ISBN-13: 978-1466461079
ISBN-10: 1466461071

Acknowledgements

Many years ago, I showed some of the stories that have made their way into this book to Lex Hixon, a magnanimous being who no longer graces this earth. Lex encouraged me to continue to expand the stories. The love that infused his comments kept me going for years.

Creating art can be a solitary and sometimes lonely pursuit. Friends and kindred spirits are essential to one's sense of purpose and well-being. I am fortunate in that regard. I have been buoyed up, inspired and brightened by many people, each of whom brings unique and wonderful qualities into my world.

Close friends Carolyn Myers and Barbara Caselli read this manuscript many times, providing helpful suggestions with kind diplomacy. Dear Neville Bayly generously supported me on many levels, opening me to new vistas. Peggy Rubin gave me an opportunity to present some of the stories at a salon during one of her Sacred Theater gatherings. Melani Marx and Sondra Bennett shared their integrative work with me in ways that stimulated my growth and creative momentum. Business consultant Gary Einhorn shared his skill and intuitive insights. Steve Scholl gave an ebullient, affirmative response to the work and has been supportive throughout.

I am grateful to each of them and to my old friends Kate Maloney, Franny Voss, Susan Bosworth, Ani Rioh and Shari Sunshine for lighting up my life with their droll humor, lovingkindness and courage.

I treasure Venerable Gyatrul Rinpoche and other Tibetan lamas from whom I have received spiritual teachings over the past 40 years. I aspire to develop the same level of compassion and selflessness that they embody.

Introduction: The Fruit of Life Ripens

There's just no accounting for happiness,
or the way it turns up like a prodigal
who comes back to the dust at your feet
having squandered a fortune far away.

--JANE KENYON

THERE'S SO MUCH ABOUT ONE'S LIFE that one does not understand until afterwards, sometimes long after. Time has to wash things over and over in its persistent waters, scouring, polishing, rubbing, smoothing down the rough edges. Then given even more time, the juiciness dries out, distilling the essence. If you live long enough, you have occasion to contemplate the meaning of events and patterns more deeply. I've had some time to do that.

I began writing this book when I was 53, during what turned out to be the last years of my second marriage. It seems odd now the way I assumed that I would always live in that funny wooden house, which was as much a carpentry experiment as a dwelling, built room by room in the 1970s by the residents of a long-gone commune called Rainbow Star. It was the kind of structure that many first-time visitors would call charming. Which I attribute to our nostalgia for the rustic life. They never tried living in that funky little place, with its odd ups, downs, nooks and crannies. It was the devil to keep clean, but even so I was fond of living there. From its windows, I gazed out into the vast mystery of the night sky, listened to the wails and howls of coyotes on nearby hills, the mating calls of the wild turkeys, sounds of tiny frogs, and the surprising snorts and bleats that deer sometimes make.

As I navigated my 50s, I contemplated my life, delving like a dowser over the terrain of memory, and writing. My writing desk faced north, looking out on a broad grassy meadow that rolled up into round hills ornamented with oak, pine and chaparral. The landscape was beautiful in its own way, but a far more wrathful terrain than the lush pastoral and soft seaside landscapes that easily attract me. In the rainy season, the dense clay soil glued itself onto your boots in 5-pound clumps, as if to say human, you are not meant to go far. In the summer, the ground dried out until it was brick-hard, but not before splitting open, revealing long angry-looking fissures.

When I sat at my desk and looked out the window towards the bottom of the meadow, I could see a 34-foot high statue of a Buddha called Vajrasattva. Vajrasattva's body was white; his garments were blue. He wore a jeweled golden crown. With his peaceful eyes and beatific smile, he sat there like a great ship from another dimension that had docked by magic in the mountain valley. Well, you may say, even if it is a very large, colorful image of a Buddha a statue is just an inanimate object. This is the way modern people tend to think.

In Tibet, the boundary between animate and inanimate, tangible and intangible, spiritual and physical, was more flexible and it was accepted that sacred statues sometimes spoke. In Tibet the presence of spiritually accomplished beings changed the landscape. Spiritual masters left footprints and handprints in solid rock. Of course, they changed the hearts and lives of flesh and blood humans, too. I know my life has been been changed by Tibetan masters. My long relationship with one Tibetan master led me to settle in that valley.

Further up the meadow at the top of the hill there was another welcome sight-- the temple called Tashi Choling, which means place of good fortune or happiness. The temple, built according to traditional Tibetan architectural standards, was a splendid, three-storied structure with white walls, red columns, and roofs colored gold. These two elements, the Vajrasattva statue and the Tashi Choling temple, altered the natural setting, opening other layers of resonance.

For many years I lived at the foot of the temple in that rustic cabin with my husband and our daughter, close to my spiritual teacher and sangha or spiritual community. But one October day I left suddenly in an awful jangle of desperation and heartbreak. My marriage exploded. How else to describe a moment when everything familiar shatters with such velocity? I mark the date my marriage exploded by recalling that a week later Princess Diana was killed in a car wreck.

I lived through the explosion, but felt like the living dead for months. And I did flee the place I assumed would always be my home. Always. Home. Assumed. These words can bring a great deal of instruction. Losing that particular refuge at the foot of the temple, along with the other losses I suffered, sundered me. When I pulled the pieces of myself back together again, I was not the same woman. Not on any level.

By the time you reach 72, which I have, you have endured various kinds of bliss, travail and loss. And you come to certain conclusions. One of the conclusions I have come to is this: no earthly home can ever take the place of what that temple means to me, to my heart. That temple, its splendor, stillness, majesty and outrageous beauty, is my real home. Don't think I am pontificating because I'm not.

And yes, I get nostalgic at times. I miss the sounds of the coyotes and the frogs. A certain lover, now long dead, a full moon night on Cape Cod...living in the fairy tale village of Bolinas. But let's face it, things were never really as great as we remember them. We burnish them and place them in our memory treasure. "Nostalgia isn't what it used to be," as satirist Peter De Vries says so well. Though sometimes nostalgia seems more like what Spanish poet Juan Ramon Jimenez wrote, "Sharp nostalgia, infinite and terrible, for what I already possess."

I spent so many years trying to find myself, trying to understand what I already embody. This seems to be a task peculiar to women. Men don't spend half as much time on it, to make a blanket statement that some men will inevitably protest. Like many other females, I lacked confidence and certainty about my identity, gifts and life purpose. Finally, through a long voyage colored with experiments in skin shedding, name changing and re-invention I found my so-called self. Let it be said again-- I found myself—hallelujah! Not only that, but I came to accept myself. I came to love myself. At this stage of life the need to try to impress anybody has been greatly reduced.

Childhood is finished, adolescence long gone, early adulthood and middle age, vanished. Yet even into my late forties,

I held onto the hope that by some special magic provided to myself alone I would escape aging, not to mention dying, that somehow, I would be borne along on the beneficent stream of time, nicely preserved at a pleasant age, say 30 or so, hair all shiny black, body slender, with the smooth skin of relative youth. What a struggle it was, surrendering that fantasy. It took years of releasing, mourning and grieving. I'm not saying it's completely done yet. But much of it has lifted off.

I find that I am content in my own company. This must be what I need at this time in my life. My daughters are grown. I've been single for 15 years, and I'm sailing into my 70s. I don't know if I will live till the morning or until I'm 80. But I do know I am in the winter of my life. And that gives everything I experience and want an edge.

The Universe continues to be generous, there is no doubt about it. I have found it worthwhile to have a sense of humor about its abundance. Once in awhile, I have the urge to go up to the top of the nearby mountain and just shout *"J'accepte! J'accepte* already!" as loud as I can, in the hope that the Universe will reconsider my case, and speaking to itself as I'm sure it does, might say, "I think she has learned her cosmic lesson, don't you?" and lighten up on the red hot lava flow it kindly sends me from time to time in its infinitely wise way. However, I suspect that I am still not finished being smelted in this particular crucible. *J'accepte, j'accepte*, smiling. *J'accepte* in whatever mood or circumstance. I am learning acceptance. So far, I have discovered that it is not pushing away. It is not giving up. It is just allowing things to be as they are.

And I have to say that there is something profoundly ironic about the long, arduous journey to find oneself, if I am any example. Because as it turns out, it's all about letting go. The day will come and I will be "laying down my mantle" as they say in gospel songs. I will have to let go of everything, the venerable old body, memories, predilections, opinions, causes, passions. It seems wise to practice now, before popping the cork.

That's why I'm offering this whole heap of stories, these songs of the inner life. Some of it may be slightly embroidered. In fact, I love embroidery. I am not an avatar of the school of photographic realism. Realism, like nostalgia, is overrated. Did it happen or didn't it happen? As a person with quite an active imagination, I often wonder myself. Here's the bottom line: If I have kept it in my memory treasure box this long, it happened. Yet, it is all a fiction. I'm a fictional character. I made myself up, just the way you did.

And we have come a long way on our journey, both of us. And perhaps we still have a long way to go.

Chapter 1   Entering the World

*"What makes the telling of personal history
stunning is that the self-disclosure of profoundly
intimate material is given with the intention of
putting oneself aside."*

--HELEN PALMER, THE ENNEAGRAM

WHEN A GIRL BABY NAMED MACHIG Labdron was born in 11th century Tibet, the third eye in the center of her forehead was open, which made some family members very nervous. One of them was so upset that she hid the baby behind a door. As if you can dispose of a being that is radiating light so easily. They had to retrieve the newborn from her odd hiding place eventually because her father wanted to see her. Observing her open third eye, he recognized that she would become a great spiritual teacher. And that is exactly what she became.

In Tibet they say that miraculous signs appear when exceptional beings are born or die. Auspicious dreams

1

are dreamed. Flowers fall like rain from the sky. Radiant displays of rainbows fill the air. Thrilling music is heard, unplayed by any human hand or mouth.

Of course then there is the rest of us, a vast river in which I myself am swimming. Some of us don't believe that life has a spiritual dimension or purpose. Some picture ourselves as victims of circumstance. Some choose the dark side. Some are so weary we can barely go on. Some are trying hard to till the ground but realize how much work there is to do before the harvest. I've spent time in each of those bardos, and I am not done yet.

I do wish I could tell you otherwise but flowers did not fall from the sky, nor did rainbows fill the air when I was born. The truth is, I didn't even want to be born. I cried incessantly for the first three weeks of my life. The gravity of earthly existence troubled me; I had a bad case of incarnational stress. My weary parents finally brought me to be seen by Dr. William Carlos Williams, who practiced medicine in nearby Paterson, New Jersey. Dr. Williams looked me over and delivered his opinion. "There's nothing wrong with this baby except that she's very hungry. Just feed her more."

I am sure that they must have followed his advice, because I have lived to tell the tale. My increased rations came in a bottle. At that time, the mother's breast was considered too intimate a part of the female anatomy to be shared with an infant. People also believed that babies should be left alone a fair amount of time, even when they cried. You didn't want to spoil a baby by giving him or her too much attention. By leaving the baby alone, the helplessly naïve creature would get toughened up, so that it could become accustomed early to being ignored or not having its needs met.

Dr. William Carlos Williams was both a physician and a well-known poet. So in its infinitely humorous and elegant way, the Universe gave me a wonderful welcoming gesture, having Dr. William Carlos Williams pop up as my baby doctor. It was my first taste of the power of healing and my first lesson on how practical and nourishing poetry can be.

"I think Dr. Williams must have thrown some poetry dust on you when you were a baby," my father said from time to time, grinning at me in his playful, affectionate way. If Dr. Williams did throw poetry dust on me, I don't remember it. I imagine that it is quite possible. Stranger things have happened. But I think it is more likely that it was my father who threw the poetry dust. My dear father, with whom I shared the love of Nature, humor, poetry and investigations into the strange and supernatural.

I doubt that my father ever read any of Dr. William's poems. His taste in poetry was more old-fashioned; he loved to recite *Hiawatha*, Longfellow's long, romantic nature poem.

Book in hand, he would take a deep breath and launch himself into that rarified atmosphere. Looking at me with his eyebrows slightly raised, reciting "the murmuring pines and the hemlocks" he transported both of us into the forest, where we breathed the vivid, moist scent of the earth and the trees. My father was not particularly well-read, but he understood the power of poetry.

Philip—that was my father's name—was a handsome man in those days: tall, slender, with laughing eyes, a wonderful nose with flaring nostrils and an elegant mouth. He was the kind of person that people describe as a free spirit. I understand why everyone thought that about him. He loved writing funny song lyrics and took great pleasure in limericks and puns. With them he not only disarmed but sometimes exhausted his listeners' laughter, patience or both. Three scents conjure my father up. The sweet aroma of the Balkan Sobrani pipe tobacco he liked to smoke, the stinky Limburger cheese he enjoyed smearing on crackers and the smell of whiskey on his breath. It's not just a straightforward piece of cake, this love they have here on Earth. I mean to say, when you love someone as much as I loved my father, who was a free spirit and also a tormented soul. We were two of a kind, as my mother liked to point out, usually in a way not intended to flatter. As I grew older, I became my father's confidante and partner in singing, joking and laughing and my mother resented our closeness. She often seemed to be a grave, disapproving presence. When I look back, nothing about her bitterness and anger is surprising. She was deeply disappointed in her marriage and her life.

I never had any compassion for her then but over sixty years later, I finally have lived long enough to understand something about what she went through. I sit here on this autumn afternoon as if she is in the room with me. We are just sitting here together. I don't have to say another word of explanation about the mistakes, confusion or sorrow of the past. We can just relax together, my mother and I, looking into each other's eyes. I am repairing my life.

Here, I have a photograph of my father, his dark hair plastered down with some kind of Brilliantine favored in those days. He sits in his comfortable upholstered chair, a picture book in his hand, smiling. He's waiting for me to climb onto his lap so that he can tell me a story.

Among the many wonderful stories my father read me, there were some he read over and over—Peter Pan, Alice's Adventures in Wonderland and Wind in the Willows among them. He also told me fantastic tales of his own invention, filled with magical, mischievous woodland characters. And now I'm telling you stories. That's how it goes, at least when fortune is with you and the blessed wind is filling your sails. You share something very precious with a person you love until finally it seems as if you have inherited it. I don't know whether what my father transmitted to me was due to genes, karmic affinity or some other kind of legacy. But I do know that these gossamer threads of the stories I'm spinning out now can be traced back to the countless tales he told me.

Entering the world—what a potent phrase. First it resonates with mystery, the mystery of where or what were we before entering the world. Then it collides with the particular details, which in my case are these: I entered the world as a Caucasian female and was given the name Gail Melissa Emaus. Gail is a shortened form of Abigail, which means her father's joy. Melissa means the honeybee, and it was the name of my father's mother. Our family name was Emaus as in Christ stopped at Emmaus, which they say he did long ago. I was born in April 1941 in the midst of what turned out to be the brief flowering of The American Dream and its strange marriage to Wonder Bread. To everyone's delight, TV appeared. Canned foods were popular and women overcooked everything except cakes and pies. People had the habit of buying a new car each year.

A terrible war was being fought when I arrived on Earth. Just think, this phrase could be employed in any modern person's life story, more's the pity for us all. The Nazis were fomenting their cruel campaign and the atomic bomb, that perversion of the Light, was being created. I entered the world in the industrial confines of northern New Jersey, which bear so many traces of the darkness Tolkein described when he wrote about the mythical land of Mordor, the land of shadows.

I wish I had pressed my mother for information about how long she labored and what her experience was in birthing me. Now it is far too late to gather that news. All I can say is that I appeared from my mother's yoni in the same way that mortals have entered the world for aeons. We all entered the world, igniting through some kind of incandescent magic. We shone like little stars, turning slowly in the dark waters of the womb. Did we know that a moment would come when we would have to leave? Did we have any memory of the rigors of the journey, how inching our way like little fish through the suffocating pressures of the birth passage, we would be pushed out irrevocably from the buoyant inner sea to the complexities of this airy world? What a gigantic and shocking transition it is to emerge into a particular epoch, culture, country, ancestral lineage, family, gender, and moment.

At least it seemed so to me. Or it would have seemed so if I could have remembered or articulated it. But I forgot everything all over again when I was born and I've been trying to remember ever since.

You may wonder why, when there are staggeringly beautiful places like Bali, Machu Picchu and the Grand Canyon available for serious earthly residency, did I fall to Earth in the murky industrial suburbs of northern New Jersey? Ah, dear reader, ah, ah. Let's get it straight right from the start. The ways of myth and the lives of goddesses are strange and mysterious, even when those goddesses are unknown to themselves.

I want to dance back a bit, to the doctor who delivered me. He cut my thick shoulder-length black hair minutes after I was born because he thought I looked too wild. Wild, as in savage, aboriginal. "Your baby's face is so red and her hair so long and black, she looks like a little Indian," he teased my mother. "Maybe you got together with a redskin."

There is some Indian blood in the family but it's on my father's side. I don't know the tribe or when Indians entered our history because the family Bible disappeared when I was young and since then nobody has taken the trouble to unearth the facts of our ancestry. I remember looking at that heavy, black, leather-bound book with my father when I was about 8 years old. On its opening pages, the family tree was recorded in a lovely old-fashioned script. As we sat there, my father pointed out to me how on his mother's side, the family, composed of Irish, English, French Huguenot and Indian blood, went back to the American Revolution. Even though I was just a kid, I could read between the lines. He was telling me that we were not mere upstarts or latecomers. We had been hard at it in America for some time, though the details of our efforts were unavailable.

After that Bible vanished, the subject was seldom raised. When it did come up, my father's face always assumed the same hurt look, followed by a dollop of consternation. "I think my brother Jim stole that Bible. I don't understand why he did it." Daddy could reliably be expected to repeat this statement, looking aggrieved at the thought that his own brother could be capable of such low, inexplicable thievery. The two of them never spoke with each other after the Bible disappeared. We still have no way of knowing how it vanished or where it might be. Without that Bible, we might as well have had no ancestors, even if on his mother's side the family tree could be traced back to the American Revolution.

If the details of the past were lost on my father's side, on my mother's side they were unmentionable. We knew one thing for a fact: my mother's mother and father came from Czechoslovakia, or maybe Hungary, because the borders shifted so much in that part of the world. But that was all we knew. What villages or towns were they born in? How did their ancestors live? Who were they? I wanted my grandfather, who looked very much like a bear, or my grandmother, who looked very much like a sparrow, to spill all those stories out. But neither Grandpa Bear or Grandma Sparrow ever said a word because they were ashamed of being recent immigrants. The subject of their origins was taboo, and their American children did not seem to care one fig about the past.

The Russian novelist Vladimir Nabokov could trace his family history back to the 1400s. Imagine that! Nobody in our family had the least interest in imagining it. Should our maternal history have been charted, would we have found the kind of aristocratic statesmen, landowners, belles dames and artists that graced Nabokov's lineage? It seems doubtful. It might actually be better not to know anything about the progenitors, their various antics and possible ignominy. That was the conclusion I finally came to during adolescence, after I had grown sufficiently acquainted with my mother's family to realize that its current members were, to put it nicely, living lives of modest circumference and depth. It would take a certain largesse to describe some of them as salt of the earth. In fact, they could have used more salt and pepper, and other spices too. They needed some of the kind of seasonings that open the heart and bring a sense of real joy. But most of them appeared to be content with their torpor, stingy jealousies and blandness.

By the time I was 7 or 8, I was sure the doctor who delivered me had been right. My real people were Indians. I wanted to be back with them. Indians or maybe gypsies—definitely dark-skinned people who lived in clans and moved from place to place on the Earth. The actual blood relatives seemed a little too pale for me. I was an Indian, and should have been out in the wilds of nature, living free. I did not belong in that stifling neighborhood of tidy small yards, trimmed hedges and narrow streets. Yet there I was, being raised white in the reservation of northern New Jersey. I bore my captivity as well as I could, which in my case involved a fair amount of resentment about a variety of things, including the tedium of school and the unfair restrictions visited on me simply because I was a girl.

For the first four years of my life, we lived in a sweet house that Grandfather Bear built. It folded around us like a bright mantle, each room light and clean, burnished by my mother's care and attention. Beautiful polished wood floors shone in the sunlight. Sun poured in through windows and curtains, throwing beautiful patterns on the walls and floor. The big walk-in pantry off the kitchen was filled with bottles and cans and home-canned jars and boxes of food, giving one the happy assurance that the next meal would definitely be forthcoming. In the damp, dim cellar with its cool earthen floors where my grandmother used to store stout barrels full of home-brewed birch and root beer, there were big coal bins and smaller bins for potatoes and onions. I liked it in the cellar. The smell of the earth and the bins and corners called to me, but I was too young to be given the freedom to explore the cellar's dark mysteries.

The neighborhood itself was quiet and slow, even bucolic by modern standards. Some houses had enormous yards ornamented by hydrangeas, lilies, roses and vegetable gardens. There were many beautiful big trees. This was where Grandpa Bear and Grandma Sparrow had raised their brood of seven kids, six of them girls. My mother Ola, who hated her given name Olga, was quite bitter about her upbringing. When I was in my teens, she described her father as an unloving, self-centered disciplinarian who dominated the house. I had always experienced my grandfather as gentle and kind, so this news was a big surprise to me.

"Father was always served first at meals," she told me. "He got the biggest portion of everything. Then John (the valued son) was served, then we girls were served. And finally our mother ate." This hierarchy troubled my mother greatly. "Mother deserved more respect, especially considering all the work she did cooking, cleaning and sewing," she told me. "John was always the favorite one," she continued, shaking her head. "It was so unfair that only John went to college." My mother never felt free enough to try to find a way to go to college herself. She maintained a lifelong belief that she would always have to settle for less than what she would have wanted, if she could have let herself even imagine what that might be. Bitterness formed a pervasive patina on her beauty.

With the exception of Babs, my mother's sisters were cautious, suspicious, stingy, sacrificially overworked women in various stages of resignation. Even my glamorous divorced Aunt Bette, who developed what my mother always described as a "career in fashion" in New York City, and included among her friends and acquaintances a variety of famous people, was plagued by terrible fear and insecurity. My Aunt Ann seemed kind but exhausted by her duties on the family farm. Aunt Irene was warm and devoutly religious, yet somehow empty and lost within. Habitually cranky Aunt Jule had an awful grating voice and sought attention by parading her obscure illnesses. Aunt Mary was the worst of them all though, vengeful and jealous as Cinderella's wicked stepmother. Those sisters formed quite a compilation. I wonder what it was like for my mother to return to live in the house where she was raised. I had none of the disagreeable associations she must have had about it; I loved that pretty stone house.

My memories of that time have the luminous sheen that gathers on childhood recollections from having been taken out and studied so many times over the years. When

I think back, it seems as if that house was our only real home. Everything that came after was just make-do, and we were like people who had been dislodged and uprooted from the real family home to wander on. I never learned why we moved from that place so that irritating Aunt Jule could move in with her husband. Like much else that was never communicated, it remains a mystery.

But none of that had happened yet and in the timeless assurance of early childhood, when each moment opens up into bright magic, I lived there with my parents as if it would last forever. I can still see the matte surface of the wooden plaques that hung on my bedroom wall and their painted images of chubby, happy children. The leaves of the maple trees made marvelous patterns on the curtains of my room as I lay down each day for my afternoon nap. How wonderful it was to have the power to conjure the attention and care of my two elegant, beautiful parents, my grandparents and various other admiring adults.

When Grandma Sparrow and Grandpa Bear moved to Florida, their visits north were a special treat. On a particular morning that stays in my memory my mother was opening the refrigerator door to get out the jar of cod liver oil. Grandma Sparrow, dressed in one of her shapeless dresses covered with tiny flowers, observed as my mother poured out the large spoonful of cod liver oil and I happily swallowed it. "She likes it, Olgy?" Grandma Sparrow asked, shaking her head in amazement. I was proud to be such an unusual, advanced type of child, one that could cause a tiny, tan, wrinkled grandmother with a wonderful accent to raise her eyebrows in surprise and appreciation.

A child finds delight and excitement in the most simple things, like the times that my father and I sat together on the stone wall at the front of the house under the big maple trees. His eyes twinkling, a bag of peanuts in one hand, my father picked me up and seated me on the wall. As I snuggled next to him, he coaxed any squirrels that happened to be nearby to come closer. His approach was so bright and welcoming, I couldn't imagine why any squirrel would not take him up on his invitation. A bit more chatting, a peanut or two cast in their direction, and soon a soft gray squirrel with bright black eyes and a quivering plumed tail was jumping up on the stone wall next to him and daintily taking a peanut from his fingers. Squirrels were very beautiful, but I was afraid of them. Once in awhile, I overcame my fear long enough to give one a peanut. Afterwards, I would invariably shudder thinking of its sharp little teeth. Whether I fed the squirrels or not, my father cocked his head and smiled at me with his twinkly eyes. Those moments of simple pleasure were very long ago. Now it's strange to remember being a child of 3, a way of being that's so different from my present existence, it's almost like another lifetime. Yet even after all those years, piercing feelings of love and nostalgia arise as I take out this memory and gaze at it. If only I could see my father once again as he was in those days, if only I could be as innocent as I was then. These memories of it are all that remain.

Expeditions with my mother were usually devoted to gathering food, attending Mass or visiting the knitting store, a place that exploded with skeins of colorful yarn and the chatter of happy groups of women, each intent on her current knitting project. My mother was an accomplished knitter. She made pretty little sweaters and dresses for me using complex stitches and patterns. I wish I kept some of the wonderful things my mother knitted for me through the years, but they all made their way into the lives of others long ago, before I knew as much as I do now about the passage of time, how it changes everything that once seemed immutable. What would it be like to have that collection of her work gathered together before my eyes today? I did not appreciate her enough.

She was so lovely. She wore delightful hats that she created herself of felt or straw, festooned with flowers or fruit, with feathers of pheasants and quails, or with veils that came down over her eyes. I adored her, though I sometimes sensed how weary my unrelenting curiosity made her. "She never stops asking questions, does she?" a woman on the bus asked her one day. "No," my mother shook her head, and a brief look of consternation passed across her face. "She never does." Now having raised two daughters of my own, I understand how she must have felt, hoping for a moment to think her thoughts, looking for a bit of time to ponder her fate. All the while there I was asking incessant questions about the bus driver, the balloon seller, and the sky. On Fridays my mother and I walked hand in hand to a shop two blocks away from our pretty stone house. At that shop, there was a Czechoslovakian man whose name I have forgotten. I will call him Radomir, which means happy peace. Radomir made delicious pierogis stuffed with prune, meat, or potato-cheese fillings. These were essential for Friday dinners, when as Catholics we did not eat meat. Once you arrived at Radomir's shop, you moved from the bright sunlight at the shop's entrance, past shelves filled with canned goods to a counter to where the pierogi maker himself, a short, good natured man with brown hair, stood smiling in the dim recesses of the back of the store, ready to fill your order for whatever quantity of those delicious dumplings you wanted to take home.

Memory is selective, quixotic and temperamental. But with all its carefully kept shrines, dark corners, buried treasures and sudden illuminations, it gives us a way to present the architecture of our soul to ourselves and to the world. Who are we if we do not remember ourselves?

In his memoir *All Rivers Run to the Sea* Elie Weisel insists, "What does it mean to remember? It is to live in more than one world, to prevent the past from fading and to call upon the future to illuminate it. It is to revive fragments of existence, to rescue lost beings, to cast harsh light on faces and events, to drive back the sands that cover the surface of things..."

It is living in more than one world. Now as I look back at my childhood from the vantage point of age, I see the truth of that. Why does one remember this but not that? Why do my brother and I remember things so differently? How does one choose one's memories? "I think it is a matter of love: the more you love a memory, the stronger and stranger it is." That is what Vladimir Nabokov opined. Do I hold all my memories in love? I wish I could say that I do. Perhaps I will hold them all in love some day, when I have fanned them with feathers, swept them with sage and juniper, and released the notion that I have any hold on them, or them on me, or that we have had anything but the most ephemeral brushes of fiction with each other. But I am not there yet. I am still in the gristmill separating the grain from the chaff. And there is as Nabokov suggests a certain kind of strong strangeness in that work.

One day in my 4th year, my mother leaned over to say goodby. We were standing in the sunny entryway of the house. I didn't understand where she was going or why. She murmured something about it, something that inferred that I would have a brother or sister soon. But I simply didn't understand. She could have been speaking Croatian. What did a brother or sister mean to me, the center of the universe? Nothing. What meant everything was that my mother was leaving me. She went out of the door and was gone. I was inconsolable. I don't remember who took care of me while she was gone. Probably one of her awful sisters. I remember being terrified, miserably unhappy and angry. Then one day, who knows how many days later, because time is not something one measures as a child, my mother returned. She came into the house with my father, and they both looked very happy. She held a little bundle of something wrapped up in blankets. She sat down with me and showed me what it was. It was alive. It was shocking. It was my baby brother. Unbelievable. Awful. But true. It is an understatement to say that I did not appreciate his arrival, which definitely ended my reign as the center of attention.

His birth also coincided with other disruptions. It seemed that his appearance marked the end of everything with which I was familiar. That sweet strong house my grand-father built, the neighbors I had come to love, the quiet, shady streets were all suddenly swept away. We moved to a ground floor flat on another street and my whiny Aunt Jule and her husband moved into the house my grandfather built. Our new street was wider. Its houses were closer together. The big trees were all clustered in the park at the end of the street.

To enter the park, you had to run past a small perfume factory that spewed a ghastly chemical pall into both the air and the stream that ran in a concrete channel through the neighborhood, behind the line of houses on our side of the street. As I grew older, I walked through the park every day on my way to school, holding my breath to lessen the effect of the chemicals, which hurt my nose and eyes. But such things as chemicals, I came to know from the adults that lived there, were part of everyday life. One had to accept them, because nothing could be done to change them.

My mother worked to paint our new house all by herself. She sewed pretty curtains decorated with sprigs of cherries for the kitchen windows. She was tired and irritable. In spite of all her efforts, the place did not have the nice feeling that our other house had. It was as if we had stepped out of a charmed fairytale into some other kind of story, though what kind of story it was did not become clear for years to come.

I have a whole series of photos of my mother that I want to show you. Here she is with a gardenia in her pompadour.

And here's my mother looking weary as she paints the kitchen cabinets in our new flat. She is painting them oyster white with red enamel handles to match the gay curtains ornamented with little sprigs of red cherries. Here's a photo of my mother bringing a sandwich and a glass of milk to one of the hobos who often passed through our neighborhood, carrying small bundles of belongings. She gave them the sandwiches and the glasses of milk and she asked them to sit on the back stoop. Then she went into the house again. I remember walking with one of those men down the street, after he had finished the lunch. It was a hot day. We sat down under a big maple tree on a hillside at the end of the block. It was right next to Larry's house. I was dying to ask him about his adventures, but I didn't dare. My mother had strictly ordered me not to question the hobos about their lives. After awhile, we said goodbye. He picked up his bundle, gave me a smile, and headed off. I went back up the street past Larry's house and Butch Katomski's house and the house where the unmarried lady and her friendly old mommy lived. The unmarried lady took me to the circus once and she gave me a beautiful bracelet from Mexico.

I passed the house where handsome Robbie Danko lived. I was in love with Robbie, a tall strapping 19-year old with dark curly hair and merry eyes. I would search for him, wearing my striped tee shirt and jeans with suspenders and pulling my hair over one eye like Veronica Lake. One day when I went to look for him, his old grandfather motioned for me to come closer. He was at the garage door. As I came towards him, he unzipped his baggy pants and took out his flaccid penis, holding it in his hand and looking at me. I turned and ran. I didn't ever go back there again, especially after I told my mother what happened and she didn't even believe me. That really hurt and a great distrust arose in me. There, I'll leave it at that.

One of the very worst days was the day my mother ran over Larry, the little boy down the street. I heard my mother hysterically yelling, telling my father over and over that Larry had run right out in front of the car. My mother said she was going very slow. How could it have happened? Yet, there was Larry with his head underneath the front wheel of the car. Everyone from the neighborhood was gathered. I was not allowed to see it. And then our house was closed in, as if we were quarantined. The shades were pulled; the curtains were shut. The priest was there every day. Crying continuously and praying her rosary, my mother stayed in bed in her dark room as the smell of the frankincense the priest offered filled the whole house. It was hard for me to understand how Larry, with whom I had been playing that day, could be alive one moment and dead the next. I was not allowed to see him with his crushed head under the wheel, or to go to his funeral.

I heard my parents talking about it. I couldn't understand why Larry's parents thought my mother was bad, why they thought that it was her fault that Larry was dead, as if she had done it on purposely. It was hard to bear my mother's suffering. I wondered if light would ever enter our house again, if she would ever smile or laugh or if she would always have the stark, afflicted visage she showed us then. I was frightened. Eventually, the priest stopped visiting. My mother grimly, wearily rose up out of her bed. We raised the shades and opened the curtains. It slowly lightened. But it was still grayish in there.

We were afflicted, all of us. It was not just because of Larry's death, though that was certainly part of it. There was much more to it. Failed dreams, distances, sorrows. It felt as if we had agreed to live underwater together, trying to shove pain under the rug, pretending that everything was perfectly normal, and acting as if death did not exist.

Today, I lit votive candles and placed them by the lovely photo of my parents when they were young and by the picture of my little brother Philip and I sitting with our mother on a wicker swing. Philip, known as Flip for most of his early life, was probably 3 years old then. He had a round face and a sweet expression. His little brown cap, short pants and jacket made him look even more adorable. He was 3, and that would make me 7. The photo shows me with a bright smile, a ribbon around my hair and jacket with white piping and a blouse with lace trim at its collar. I was terribly jealous of my brother, but he was really a darling kid.

We had the standard two-child family popular at that time, so different from the seven kids in my both my mother's and father's families. My father grew up in a tall angular Victorian house on Anny Goat Hill in Paterson, New Jersey. Perched on a steep piece of land, that house always seemed as if it was being squeezed on each side by unseen forces intent on compressing it and pushing it up to the heavens. When I was a child, my Aunt Phoebe was the curator of those small, dark rooms, which were crowded with many years of family relics and mementos. The place always had a gothic flavor to me, but Phoebe somehow remained quite jolly there.

Both of my father's parents died by the time he was 10. They were Dutch Baptist ministers, religious with a vengeance. The one photograph I have shows them with all seven of their children. That photo is the only way I have met my father's parents or siblings, so I have looked at it many times. It is summer. A tree and rosebush throw leafy shadows on the shed behind them. There's laundry hanging on a line. Probably sheets. A chicken wire fence behind the family group completes the backdrop. My grandparents seem rather forbidding. Grandfather Cornelius is pale with weary circles under his eyes and doughy looking cheeks. I think he looks worried, worn out, irritated. A tall man with broad shoulders, he wears a dark jacket that appears to be too large. He tilts his head to the right. On his lap he holds moon-faced Lucy, who must be about five.

When I look at Grandmother Melissa, it makes me think that the Indian blood might not be far back at all. Her skin is quite dark. A sturdy looking woman with fierce, wary eyes, she wears her hair pinned up, ornamented with a dark bow. Her beautiful mouth rests in a grim expression. On her lap she holds a baby who must be about 3 months old. It's my father. The oldest child, Allie, about 13, stands behind her mother. Next to her is the dark-skinned Nelly, looking truly forlorn despite her bright gingham dress. Phoebe, smiling and cheerful, sits next to Nellie. The suspected Bible thief James stands behind Grandfather Cornelius. Cornelius Jr. stands on the other side of his father, looking like a boy who has already learned something about being sneaky.

If you're a minister the way my grandfather was, you have a mission, the job of saving people's souls and bringing them to eternal salvation. Weak and sinful, they stray far from the fold, ignoring their immortal souls. Bringing them back and saving them is a serious business. You might feel the need to work with a vengeance, using a hellfire and brimstone kind of approach. I think my grandfather and grandmother probably conducted their ministry that way. According to my dad, they conducted their parental duties with a vengeance, too. Their mission was clear: those children would be saved.

"In church all day on Sunday, every Sunday," my father once told me. "We were not allowed to move. If we moved, we were hit. They just tried to beat the hell out of us, and thought it would make us be religious. There was not much love in that house and not much of any real religion either," he said. Because of his punishing upbringing, my father had deep distrust of organized religion. "I'm a pantheist," was how he explained himself. "Nature is my church." It was important to my mother for me to be baptized as a Roman Catholic and I was. On my baptism certificate, my father was listed as a Heathen. He always found that very amusing.

I never knew most of those relatives in the photograph. What kind of lives did they live? What were their gifts and downfalls? What about their medical history, a subject you begin to think about when you grow older. All unknown. I come back to the baby, my father. His hands are curled up on his ferocious mother's lap and he is looking out at the photographer with a puzzled expression on his face. Or perhaps it's just that the sun was in his eyes.

Something gothic happened in the family house. My mother told me about it when I was 15. "Don't let your father know that I said anything about this to you," she insisted. So I added one more parental secret to my collection of items one parent told me, urging me not to tell the other one. It was a tragedy, that much I could see from her face. Turned out to be the way some tragedies are: short and violent. My father's oldest sister Allie was discovered having sex with a man in her bedroom of the family house. Unable to bear the shame, she hanged herself soon after in that same room. Maybe it was my father who found her. Even before my mother told me about Allie's death, I felt the darkness in that house. Aunt Phoebe's cheerful presence camouflaged it somewhat, but the ripples and eddies of the suicide and the children's pain and anger still roamed sadly through that structure.

It doesn't matter that I never even knew any of them except Aunt Phoebe and my father. Looking at that photograph of my father's parents and siblings, I feel for them. All of them suffered through life's various epiphanies and tribulations; all of them died. I keep them in my prayers, along with all my long-unseen cousins, and the surely now-deceased aunts and uncles.

When I became a Buddhist 40 years ago my ideas about ancestry expanded. Buddhism suggests that in the course of our countless lifetimes all beings have been our parents. Countless lifetimes, imagine that. That means my kinfolk are everywhere, in all countries, world systems and periods of times. I find it possible to embrace this vision. However, like a lot of other human beings, I have found my blood relations and those I love the most are among the most confounding, loveable and heartbreaking of all.

"And you shall die beloved dust and all your beauty stand you in no stead," Edna St. Vincent Millay wrote some decades ago. This is a difficult, inescapable part of life. Both my mother and father have passed away. My father died when I was 32; my mother died about 10 years later. Now my brother and I are the only ones left who share memories of the time we spent together. The last time I saw my mother, she was asleep in a hospital bed; her eyelids seemed nearly transparent. Within three months of my visit, she died. I could do nothing to save her. I wanted to save her. I wanted to save them all, all those loved ones who have died: my father, my mother, Jerome, Kate, dear Al and Miguel. But all of them died. There was nothing I could do. It is only a matter of time until I face the death of more dear friends and kin, unless I die before them.

Aging gives everything more of an edge. From my current vantage point, feeling quite vividly alive yet sensing the pull of my own demise, I sometimes find myself soaring up over my life. The view is panoramic and there's a certain detachment and tenderness that comes along with it. I find myself looking at events, people, places and the passage of time itself the way an old person watches children at play. Florida Scott-Maxwell said it beautifully, noting that in later life one has "time to face everything one has had, been, done, gather them all in: the things that came from outside, and those from inside. We have time at last to make them truly ours."

People sometimes use the phrase "living in the past" in an accusatory way, as if the process of recollecting and investigating the meaning of one's life is something infantile, rather than a profound exploration. As one grows older, it's natural to reflect on one's life and to search for its meaning, to focus more on being rather than on doing and to spend time going within. This is a big part of the developmental work of the later years.

I'm glad that others my age are getting into the inner life because it's been such a long time preoccupation of mine. For as long as I can remember, I have found the inner life at least as compelling as the outer life. My fascination with the intangible worlds of imagination and spirit put me at odds with the velocity and wildly productive thrust of modern life, which is so obsessively focused on material events and substances. I would have been more at home with the slower pace and broader intellectual style of the early Renaissance. At that point in time, nobody found it unusual if a person painted, wrote poetry, speculated about the nature of the universe and also built beautiful furniture when the spirit moved her. Renaissance people didn't have the pressure that we have to specialize in one thing.

However, we are not living in the Renaissance and I had to deal with the fact that I was living in the contemporary industrial era whose pervasive atmosphere poet Ezra Pound so aptly described when he wrote *"The age demanded an image of its accelerated grimace."* That comes down to a certain amount of grimacing being done by all of us, for our sophisticated technologies seems to be glued together by the uneasy tensions and dislocations of the humans running them. I will spare you the rest of my rant on this particular subject for the time being and simply confide something we all know: society exerts expectations and demands on each individual in it, insisting that we conform to its preferred style and values.

In other words, one must adapt to circumstances. This can be somewhat shocking, which explains why as children many of us assumed that we had been dropped by mistake into the wrong family, era, race or gender. After awhile though, we all realized we were going to have to grapple with our disappointment and adapt somehow.

For decades, I swear I did my best to acclimatize to the accelerated grimace. However, when I look back at it, I believe I overcompensated. Was it really necessary to fly around like a hornet in the manic Type A lifestyle I lived for so many years?

Reflecting the kind of person I was earlier, I am reminded of how little I understood about myself or the power I had to manifest and create my life. It never occurred to me that I could forge my own unique way and be comfortable about it. It took decades to come to that realization. Instead, my way of adapting was to take up our society's most valued behaviors. The safest way to act, it seemed to me, was like a man. So I disguised myself as an aggressive, competitive, hurried, achievement-driven, impatient Type A woman. The disguise worked so well that after a few years passed, I was well disguised even from myself.

I can't say that I regret being the way I am, or the way I was, even though it has taken me quite awhile to drop the disguises and mature into myself. Nor do I wish I were more enamored with the speedy mechanized ways of the modern world, which some people actually seem to believe is the apex of human achievement. I heard a politician on the radio the other day who sounded very much like a preacher. He was yelling fervently "America is the best and most advanced culture ever known in the history of the world!" Some listeners may have been impressed. To me, it was pathetic. The most advanced culture ever known in the history of the world? Come now.

In the modern world, we are indoctrinated to rely upon measurable empirical evidence and to distrust the workings of the imagination and the invisible realms of resonance, spirit and energy as quixotic, inefficient or unfathomable, leading a person who knows where, but surely somewhere impractical and even dangerous. What a terribly limited perspective. The facts just don't go far enough because the visible world is only a small part of the experience we find ourselves moving through. Relying merely on empirical evidence reduces everything, leaving out essential, powerful elements like poetry, chaos and miracles. What about opening up everything we assume as real to broader inquiry, to the songs of the inner life with its dreams, synchronicities and surprising insights, meetings and events?

It's popular to talk about factors like gender, race, sexual preferences, nationality and place as reasons why someone turned out the way they did. Of course, all of those elements had their impact on me. But none of them orchestrated my penchant for the inner life. For that, I hold the stars and planets responsible. You see, I was born at the dark of the moon, a time just before the new moon, when the silvery lunar orb dissolves into the vastness of the night sky and the veil between the visible and invisible worlds thins. I imagine that's why resting in the dark comforts me so deeply. I love night's vast stillness, the expansive feeling of oneness that rises when everything sleeps. Under cover of darkness, the obstinate details of ordinary earthly life are obliterated; one can forget their pull for awhile.

The Universe gave me a double dose this lifetime, bestowing upon me not only the dark of the moon gift, but offering in addition a celestial map that includes six planets in the twelfth house. This is like taking a long journey into two countries with similar languages and culture, because both the dark of the moon and the twelfth house represent doorways into the personal and collective unconscious, pipelines into unseen archetypal and spiritual dimensions. Both are associated with healing and psychic sensitivity.

Of course, this was not something recorded in my soft pink baby book, where my birth weight and length were carefully written, and my little handprint indicated that I had arrived on Earth. If I had been born in India or Tibet, my parents would have asked the local astrologer to draw up my natal chart. As it was, I didn't learn anything about what the stars and planets had to tell me about the deeper meaning of my life until I was 30 years old. I wish I could have retrieved this information sooner. But it seems unlikely that it could have happened earlier. I was meant to be in the dark for a long time. Feeling my way around in the dark was the way I learned.

Astrologers used to describe the 12th house as a nasty, shadowy place of confinement, hidden enemies, self undoing, past life debt and unfinished karmic business, using phrases like "the valley of miseries," "the dark den of sorrow and horror," the "portal of toil." I remember one astrologer looking at me aghast when I told her I had 6 planets in the 12th house, as if I had revealed I was Rasputin. "You've got 6 planets in the 12th house?" There was a sharp intake of breath, a rolling of the eyes, and unspoken but clearly communicated pity for my sorry-ass doomed predicament.

However, we do live in a world of polarities, which includes two sides of the same coin and fluctuating opinions. So there are very different ways of viewing things, including the 12th house. It's only fair to speak about the positive aspects of the 12th house, which is the last house in the astrological wheel and represents a commitment to spiritual development and a natural immersion in the inner life. Hey lady, will it be confinement or liberation? Sorrow or joy? I'll just say that after living seven decades, I am well aware of how in one person, in this case myself, both predator and mystic can live side by side.

Now it's time for my disclaimer. Despite this moon phase and astrology orientation, I am not a woo-woo type of person. The Urban Dictionary describes woo-woo as "descriptive of an event or person espousing New Age theories such as energy work, crystal magic, Reiki, bizarrely restrictive diets, or supernatural/paranormal/psychic occurrences," giving as an example, *"She's so woo-woo she put a rose quartz crystal and Bach Flower Essences in her cat's water dish."* I have never done that with the cat's water dish, not that I recall. As you can see from the Urban Dictionary's take on woo-woo, involvement in energy work, crystals, paranormal events and Eastern religions is regarded as rather odd and off the beam, as opposed to things like geekiness, driving a Rolls Royce, or keeping large amounts of money in offshore accounts. My natural inclinations, gender and sensibilities have allowed me to play out my life in counterpoint to the dominant cultural paradigm. Perhaps I should utter a loud Hallelujah here. Yes, I believe I will. It doesn't matter to me if you decide I am woo-woo, either.

The ancient Greeks, who were famous for their attention to the art of memory, maintained that it is easier to remember the grotesque than the beautiful. I wonder about this, but it does seem that there is an element of the grotesque in some of the keenest memories from my childhood years. For instance, I had two recurring nightmares. The first happened when I was very young, as I lay in the darkness at the threshold between sleep and waking. Each night, I was filled with dread, wondering whether the door would open again and light pour in from the hallway, breaking open the safe envelope of darkness. Inevitably, each night just as I feared, the door opened and the light poured in, illuminating my small body on the bed. Then the door shut again very quietly, nearly all the way. Now only a little light was left. In that dim light large, dark, silent beings approached slowly and stealthily, never speaking or uttering a sound. When they reached my bedside, they stood over me, their presence enormous and dangerous. I was sure they had come to kill me. Completely terrified, I lay with my sheets and blankets pulled up over my head and I remained as still as death, hoping that they would think I had vanished. This happened night after night. It was only many years later that I had a great insight; it occurred to me that those dangerous and enormous beings must have been my parents, coming to tuck me in. And do I have an explanation for you about why this terrified me so? No, I do not. Was it something from a past life? It could have been. And though it had quite an influence on me as a young child, now it no longer compels me. These days I have other fears and tangles to work on.

In the second recurring nightmare, which happened while I was asleep, I stood on a sandy beach while all about me an immense storm raged. I was completely alone. When I looked out to sea, I saw a great wave gathering on the horizon. It came speeding across the ocean toward me, gigantic and deadly. It gathered monstrously over me, rising up, forming an inconceivably huge arc over me. And then it froze. I was paralyzed with fear, looking up at its unmoving massive contours, waiting for it to crash down over me.

I don't remember ever telling anyone about these two difficult experiences. Dreams were never included as a valid topic of discussion in our family. Accepting without question that dreams were somehow not appropriate to share, I lived two lives, the outer life and the inner life, and my inner life, which was very rich, remained locked inside me like a secret treasure. The only one who ever examined its surprising contents, puzzling over their meaning, was me. Although my inner life during childhood was quite terrifying at times, I do consider it a treasure, filled as it was with arcane emblems and figures that led me forward into deeper understanding.

Some themes and questions persist or repeat, and this is part of the puzzle we are given in human life. One day when I was 42 I came across a book on tidal waves in a bookstore. A photograph taken in Japan sent chills through me. A tiny figure stood transfixed, staring up at an immense wave that was about to sweep down to end his life. There was nothing he could do. I stood there for a long time, breathing and looking at the picture, close to tears. The experience of looking at that photo was like being out of the body and looking down at life from another vantage point. That place and event were piercingly familiar. Was that my death? That's exactly how it felt.

The fear and dread that pervaded both those childhood nightmares had an archetypal quality, as if they came from other lives or dimensions. And they may have. But fear and dread were also part of my everyday life. There was a dark undertow in our family. My father was drinking and he was ashamed of it. My mother was disappointed and angry. Both tried to hide their discord from us, but my brother and I felt it keenly. I did not feel safe.

Photographs come to mind, ones I have not looked at in years. There's a picture of my little friend Shirley with a delighted expression on her face as we blew bubbles into the air. I remember the moist green hillside in her back yard where we ran around playing tag near a big patch of rhubarb by the brook. There's a photograph of me wearing a striped shirt and jeans, a gun and holster around my waist, an Indian headband at my forehead, a plastic flower behind my ear and a bright look in my eyes as if to say, "Now this is more like it." I also have a picture of Butch Kotomski with his crew cut and a big grin. I wonder where Butch Kotomski is now. I wonder what life has brought him and Shirley and the others I played with so many years ago.

Sometimes it seems strange to me that there are no photographs of two of the most important characters in my childhood. Even though they are both *agentes imagines,* elements of my imagination, each had a lasting influence on my life. I suppose you could call the first one a secret friend, the kind of magical friend that children sometimes have. Perhaps I imagined him, but he was very real to me. His skin was golden, his hair long and silvery. He was old, but his body was supple. He wore only one garment that wrapped like a short skirt around his lower body. He was very different from anyone I knew in so-called real life, yet nothing about him surprised me. He seemed familiar, as if he had always been there in my awareness. When my heart hurt too much from the ominous undertow of sorrow and conflict that darkened our home, I set off to see him. These expeditions took place in my imagination, yet they were vivid enough to remain in memory all these years, when many other more mundane events of what we consider real life have dissolved into dust.

He lived in a stone cave near the sky. To get there, I had to climb high into snow-covered mountains. I don't know what mountains they were; but they were certainly far bigger than any peaks I had ever seen in New Jersey, where there are no real mountains at all. The snow on their formidable expanses shone brilliantly in the sun. Finally, I came face to face with him, sitting on a rock ledge at the front of his cave as if he had been there for ages. I clambered up the final few steps to the stone surface and sat next to him. We never spoke, but the silence we shared, expansive and full of light, was worth more than any conversation that took place far below. Many nights I fell asleep up in those brilliant snowy mountains, though to all outer appearances it seemed that I was lying peacefully in my bed at home.

I never told anyone about the hermit. I did not dare to speak of him, because that experience, sitting next to him on the floor of the cave, as the vast sky blazed with brilliant motes of light, as the snow radiated rainbow colors and a perfect peaceful stillness filled all of space, was too precious to expose to the ridicule that I feared would erupt if I mentioned even a word about him. It was then that I began to grapple with the distinctions between what is real and what is unreal. The mountain hermit was the deepest, most reliable, most truly real human being I knew. I wanted everyone to see his kind eyes and to feel the peace of his presence. I wished that his radiance would permeate our entire house, working its magic in our family, and that it would shine through the dismal war and the sorrow people carried in their faces and bodies. But, though I pondered it mightily, I could find no bridge over which to bring him forth from the invisible into the visible world.

Who was he? I don't know. I have no name for him even now. Where did he come from? I don't know. Why did he appear? Again, I do not know. As a child, none of that mattered to me. It did not seem in the least bit odd to travel up the snow-covered mountain to sit near him. I was a child, and children, unconfined by logic, are free to embrace the world of the imagination as real. And he was very real to me, that mountain hermit, yogi or whoever he was. He was a great source of strength and joy. With him, I felt peaceful and whole.

In the midst of this, I grew older, and ordinary reality exerted its pull. It became more difficult for me to reconcile the hermit's presence with the circumstances of my everyday life. He, after all, was a figment of my imagination and I was a Catholic girl living in northern New Jersey, far from massive snow mountains or golden hermits. I took one step backwards and then another and another, moving out of the realm of his radiance until I drowned in the visible world. I did not have the strength or understanding then to do anything else. That's how the mountain hermit faded and was gone. Something truly marvelous and nurturing died in me, and there was not even a funeral. No one even knew that there had been a death. Even I didn't know, doing my best to eradicate all traces of his presence in my efforts to conform to the expectations of the outer world.

When the mountain hermit vanished, I was more alone than ever. We had moved again, this time into a top floor flat on another street. There was a big mulberry tree in the yard and the school was right across the street. My mother recruited my brother and I to help her paint the living room and dining room walls a horrible green color that looked like pea soup. I can't imagine what she enjoyed about this color, which cast an uneasy pallor. It was too yellow to be at home with the softer green color of the couch and chairs. When the time came to put slipcovers over the living room furniture, the color of the walls seemed at odds with their fabric, too, clashing with both the yellow of the flowers and the green of the leaves.

My mother always aspired to have a beautiful, peaceful home. That's why she exerted herself to paint each new place afresh. I am sure she didn't realize when she chose that green color for the walls that she was painting our house in a way that described the colors of our distress. We started out losing our mooring and being adrift. Then we came to spells of cold days and rough waters. By the time we moved into this third house, we were hanging on for dear life. The wind was whipping. The boat was thrown high into the air on huge waves, then dropped with dreadful force as the waves crashed.

Among ourselves we endured these storms without comment as if they were not happening. I discovered one day that we all were actually living underwater, walking through the rooms painted the color of cream of pea soup like drowned mariners. At times the storm passed, and we had a respite to come up for air, but soon we found ourselves back in the boat, desperately clinging to its weakening boards while the endless waters of the sea crashed around us. In that bleak landscape, I wanted to run away. I wished things were normal. But nothing was normal in our house—and I was not normal.

My own body betrayed me, marking me as someone with a dark secret. It was my left foot. It was deformed. The toe next to the pinky was missing a joint. It looked normal until I was about seven years old. Then one day in a bakery at the beach, a little boy pointed to my foot and loudly asked his older brother, "What's the matter with her toe?" Mortified, and covering my left foot with my right foot, I couldn't wait to get out of there. Not long after, I asked my parents accusingly, "What's wrong with my toe—that one there?" They looked at each other, dismayed. So much was in that look. I was mentioning the unmentionable. It was like referred pain, the way my question pointed to everything else that could not be acknowledged. Then they smiled and told me, "There's nothing wrong with your toe. It's perfectly all right." I didn't believe them, and I don't think they believed themselves. Nothing was all right, including my left foot.

Perhaps they thought they could pacify my mind, the way adults do when a child gets a scrape, and they say, "There, there, it's nothing. It will be better soon." But our conversation was different from that. There was no acknowledgement of my wound. In fact, I was told I had no wound. That little toe was the symbol of everything that needed healing in myself, and at least in that instant, everything that needed to be healed in my family.

Recounting this to you, it seems like another life, and in many ways it was. My deformed little toe, tiny though it may be in the cosmic sweep of things, was the occasion of much anxiety and grief for many years. Nevertheless, I have come to understand that my left foot is in certain ways my best foot. What have I learned from my right, supposedly normal, foot compared to everything my left foot has taught me? This is not entirely fair to my right foot, which I must admit has supported me in all normalcy my entire life. Extended nakedly to public gaze, it has evoked no stir whatsoever, moving with perfect aplomb through everything. It has never questioned or been questioned.

These days I think that my little toe is a great storyteller and teacher. Materializing out of nowhere as part of my left foot, it has been a patient companion, even in the midst of my determined rejection. Love yourself, my tiny toe said to me, accept yourself as you are. Do I appear to be something unformed, unborn, something only dimly remembered? Then form me, bring me to birth, sing my truths. When I think of everything that I have experienced through the grace of my little toe, I wonder if my feet had been as lovely as Aphrodite's, would they ever have spoken to me so eloquently? It's obvious from the way I ask the question what I think the answer is.

But it was another story entirely during my childhood. Then that little toe was a sign of how bad I was. I didn't want anyone to know how bad I was. I had something to hide, so I began to hide it. I couldn't let it show. I didn't want anyone to see it. I didn't want to be singled out. I didn't want them to call me awful names. They might ridicule me. All that was bad enough but there was something worse, and that was the difficult matter of the dark things under my bed. They were terrifying and malevolent. They wanted to hurt me because I had that shameful toe, because I was bad. I was deformed. There was something evil about me.

If I didn't have that toe, the dark things would have no hold on me. If I wasn't evil, and if I didn't have that toe to prove it, my family would be happy. It was all my fault. Even so, I had to protect myself from the dark things. So every night I continued the battle with the dark things under my bed. One night something really terrible happened. I have no idea how they did it, how all the little dark things, which were awful enough when they were under the bed, telescoped into one big dark thing. A monster. He rose up on two legs, black and hairy, with terrifying fangs, eyes and claws. I had to use every bit of my mental energies and my will to keep him at bay, forcing him back into the closet. It was exhausting.

Logically, I knew that the monster was not real, yet on another level he seemed completely real to me, frighteningly real. When I was alone in my room, he would appear at the slightly open closet door, roaring silently, with his mouth gaping open and those fangs of his looking very scary.

"No, you cannot come any further," I would insist mentally. "You must go back." He was fearsome, heavily armored, relentlessly aggressive. He meant to do me in. Then the battle would begin in earnest as I used my will to push him back into the closet. This went on for years. Now I can say these five words as if they are any sequence of harmless five words in the language. This went on for years. About 20 years.

Finally it ended. There were no fireworks, no apocalyptic finale. He simply began to fade from my imagination. The story lost its grip on me. It was around the time when I first began to meet and study with Tibetan spiritual masters, beings who came from the Land of Snows, whose immense mountain ranges are so like the mountains where my secret friend the mountain hermit lived. Ah, what a wonderful coincidence that is.

I am very glad that I no longer battle the dark monster. But the hallucination of his monstrous rage strengthened me. He helped me to face myself. He filled my imagination and left me shaking in terror like a skeleton rattling in search of something reliable. So many years of struggle, contemplating a battle frozen in time. Finally, I had to ask myself, is he really anything other than me? I had to look at him with new eyes. What will make him happy? He was so alone and afraid. Who would ever have guessed, seeing his massive fierceness, just how small and vulnerable he really was? So I befriended him at last. I assured him that he was mine and I was his. I would not abandon him or cast him out. I asked him to reveal his secrets.

I wonder at times whether the hermit in the mountain cave sent the dark monster to rouse my spirit when I stopped climbing up to visit him on the mountain. I wonder whether the dark monster was the hermit in another form, engaging me in a deep struggle, the beginning of spiritual work. The dark beings, the gigantic tsunami wave, the mountain hermit, the bad toe and the dark monster. What a strange cast of characters, and what strange themes some of them illuminated. I do not pretend to understand how or why they arose in my imagination or why I perceived them as I did. But I have come to appreciate these vivid way stations of my journey. For each of them was a way station.

Chapter 2   Gypsy Traces

Dewdrop, let me cleanse
in thy brief sweet waters
these dark hands
of life.

--BASHO

TO BE A SUCCESSFUL WHITE HUMAN in the New Jersey suburbs, if one believed some of my mother's sisters, a person
(and especially a female) had to cultivate a state of vigilance
against those dark and passionate creatures, the gypsies.
But naturally I did not agree. When I thought of gypsies,
I heard scintillating music. Cascades of feeling and color
surged through my body. By the age of 8, I was convinced
that if I could only get a pair of gypsy boots, they would
carry sufficient magic to walk me through the mundane veil
of northern New Jersey into another, richer landscape, and
as you may have guessed, that was something I definitely
wanted to do. With me, if it wasn't Indians, it was gypsies.

Anyway, how could I discard gypsies from my imagination when both my parents embraced them? My father for instance had a persistent fantasy of driving off in a gypsy wagon. On Sundays, when because of some Sabbath truce the fighting between my parents could be set aside for a few hours, my father took us for meandering drives along back roads in the country and regaled us with his plan to trade in his Chevy for a gypsy wagon painted in brilliant colors, to be drawn by a lovely team of horses. Lulled by the movement of the car, the good feeling between my parents, and the refreshing countryside, it was easy to imagine that this was a possible future. One day we would wake up and pile into that gypsy wagon, a vehicle that spoke vividly of our wilder dreams. Leaving the suffocating, tidy little neighborhood behind, we would free ourselves of that denatured suburban life for good. It took the edge off, added a splash of hope and color.

My mother had her own gypsy secrets. One day when she took me with her to the Russian Tea Room in New York City, I caught a glimpse of them. I don't know how much of what I remember about the Russian Tea Room is real, and how much I have embroidered over the years. The threads of memory and imagination when taken up over and over, woven, unwoven, then woven again, can lose some of their original quality. Fibers intermingle and become dreamlike. Lures of the imagination tinkle like an enchanted bracelet at the wrist. In other words, do not be surprised if when you go to the Russian Tea Room, the Russian dancing bears made of faceted crystal that I describe here are not part of its decor.

From the street, the tearoom did not appear to be anything out of the ordinary. But as we walked up the stairs, the first traces of violin music sent their tendrils out to greet us. I felt timid about going through that big doorway, its heavy iron ornamentation fashioned into rococo curves. The place was as elegant as a big cathedral I had seen once, and a lot more lively. I was in heaven there because the Russian Tea Room was home to a small tribe of gypsy men with colorful bandanas tied around their heads. Just their bandanas and their vests, beautifully patterned with paisley, diamond shapes and flowers, were enough to seduce me into another reality. Their white shirts had sleeves that ballooned out as the sleeves of no conventional man may do. Their pants ballooned out too, then dove inside the tops of their high black boots. Their hair was dark and curly, and their black eyes shone as they wandered through the rooms playing heartbreaking songs on their violins. I didn't recognize any of the melodies they played that day except one called *O Cichonya*, which my father sang all the time. In English it went *O dark eyes of fire/ grant my one desire/ my sweet gypsy dove/ give me all your love.* I may be misremembering the actual lyrics, but I do know that in the midst of everyday life with its fighting, drinking and money problems, my father courted my mother with that song. Opening the invisible doorways hidden in ordinary rooms with *O Cichonya*, he stepped through into the fragrance of jasmine, into the music and soft night air that envelope lovers and sends them floating through the sky entwined with each other as they do in Chagall paintings. His nostrils flared as he sang. His eyes were laughing. My mother looked at him with a little smile as the scent of the jasmine reached her and he drew her through the invisible doorway with him. I saw this happen. So I knew the magic of gypsies early on.

My mother and I walked through a series of rooms with high ceilings and walls covered with wine colored brocade. Samovars of copper, brass, and silver sat on tables, sideboards and counters. Lamps with amber shades were set into niches on the wall. It was a place redolent with ancestral spoor. No matter that my mother's family was not Russian, but Czechoslovakian and Hungarian. This detail was not important to my mother and I. We trafficked in the glory of old Russia as the intense, sad eyes of familiar nobles gazed out at us from huge paintings framed in rococo gilt. Finally we were seated at a table with a small bouquet of bright flowers. I was lost in the tearoom's exotic splendor. Only my mother's beauty anchored me. From the delicious display of samovars, mysterious portraits, flowers, lamps, brocade, crystal bears, and vivid gypsy men, my attention eventually returned to her. I remembered that I was the daughter of this distant, exquisite woman with pearly skin and dark hair, her lovely profile framed in the sunlight that came in through the windows, her graceful hands resting on the white cloth of the table. The setting brought her out. That afternoon in the Russian Tea Room, my mother showed herself to me in all of her natural grace and kindness and in all her unlived potentials. Thinking of that moment again, remembering her innocence and despair brings tears to my eyes for my mother and for every mother who sacrifices or stifles her dreams or whose lives are so encumbered that they never dare to dream at all. We sipped tea from pretty cups and nibbled on sweets set on delicate little plates.

Our everyday china was clumsy compared to those plates. The routines of our daily life were dull compared to the gorgeous rituals of the tearoom where every moment over-flowed with music, vivid color and passion. Why could we not live in this splendid heightened world every day? Even if I knew how to frame the question then, I would not have dared to ask it aloud.

My mother beckoned for the woman who read tea leaves. I think that the reader should have been wearing a deeply fringed triangular silk shawl profusely embroidered with flowers. She needed a beautiful mantle to reassure us that her thin fortune-telling music was every bit as wonderful as the music of the whole gypsy orchestra. But as it was, she wore a common, rather matronly dress. Arranging herself at our table, she picked up my mother's teacup and swirled the tea leaves with an expression of grave concentration. My darling mother was so dear and so unhappy. Even as a child, I knew that she hoped for some miracle of release and transformation.

People want to believe that children are impermeable as little stones, even when scoured with the torrents of adult passion that flow over and around them. But children are not impermeable. They breathe everything in. I was no different from any other child in that way. I knew the identity of many dangerous longings, though I could not have spoken of them then. The woman swirled the leaves again and again as if to clarify their meaning. Then she told my mother that she would be meeting a tall, dark handsome man, granting my mother this hackneyed fortune-telling cliche. My mother glanced at me, uneasy for a moment that I had become privy to such intimate details of her life. But as the lure of the fortuneteller's message drew her back, she seemed to forget that I was there. She grew excited. Was the tall, dark handsome man her husband? she asked the reader. Did this reading signify a renewal of their love? The tea leaf reader looked at my mother's face. Was it pity I saw in her eyes? She shook her head slowly. It is not your husband, she told my mother. It is another man. You will meet another man. I wanted to scream. My heart was pounding in my chest. Why was there such pity in the reader's eyes? What about my Daddy?

My mother looked exhilarated. Her cheeks were flushed. Her eyes darted here and there like a creature set loose in a wonderful new territory. She asked the reader other questions. When would she meet this man? How would they meet? Would she leave her marriage for him? The dull thud of her questions landed like bullets inside me. My mother, however, was buoyant. At that moment she seemed like a woman already in love. On our way home, however, she composed herself, which is to say that she sank back down into her habitual reserve and resignation. She cloaked herself.

We never visited the Russian Tea Room together again. I return there in imagination from time to time to gaze at the beautiful men in the gypsy orchestra, to bask in my mother's beauty for a few moments, and with the smell of her perfume close by, to sip a quiet cup of the black tea of memory. I have no idea whether she ever met the tall dark handsome man. There are so many things about my mother I never knew because of the way she hid herself away. She made herself small and placed herself in a long clear bottle where she lived, an intricate, beautiful model of a sailing ship whose sea voyages, if they occurred, were never described to me. I wish she had taken more risks. I wish she had shared more of herself. I wish she had done more of what she truly wanted to do.

I found the gypsy boots when I was 17, put them on and walked through the veil that separates New Jersey from other more exotic worlds. I was a free spirit, as free as anyone can be in this complicated world. Those boots became very comfortable, almost as good as being barefoot. I have worn them in many different geographies, both inner and outer. They are more a state of mind than a pair of boots by now.

The gypsies began to travel away from their homeland in India about 1,000 AD, and the reasons for their long, wide migration are still mysterious. Were they were forced from their original home because they stole children, robbed horses and in general caused criminal mischief? Or were they impelled to set off by some other, more cellular nomadic impulse? Nobody really knows. To a person like me, confined in industrial culture and suburban routines, the wandering life of gypsies seemed enormously attractive. Of course, my view of them was as romantic as my view of Indians. I never looked at the awful difficulties that gypsies or Indians face. I took only the most colorful parts and ignored the rest. Gypsies and Indians had freedom to move around in Nature, and that was what I longed for. You'd think that by now, I might have camped out in a gypsy wagon in open fields for a summer or two, or danced in firelight with bangles on my ankles. But so far I never have. Which is not to say that I never will. It still could happen, because I am still alive and the magical display of life is still unfolding in marvelous and unpredictable ways. Yes, it could still happen.

I've had my own migration route and its circumference has been far more modest than that of a bona fide gypsy. At 17, I traveled to New York City, which was only about 20 miles but a world away from the city in northern New Jersey where I was raised. In Manhattan, I moved from place to place for 11 years. Some years I moved every 3 or 4 months; other years only once. I guess it can be counted as some kind of odyssey, though it lacks the kind of dramatic sweep most travel adventures have. Especially because my friends were traveling to exotic places like India, Morocco and Paris. Travel didn't exert any pull on me then. I just moved from place to place in New York City.

One large, sunny ground floor room I lived in when I was 18 had the spacious, welcoming feel of a farmhouse kitchen. Light streamed in through three very tall windows, the kind you see in old Parisian buildings. Worn linoleum floors disclosed underlying layers of earlier linoleum archaeologies.

The ceiling was covered with embossed tin squares that had been painted white. On the old iron bedstead, the bright silk squares of my grandmother's comforter seemed quite at home. My kitchen table, placed in the middle of the room, also served as a desk. The heat and hot water were reliable, cockroaches seldom appeared due to the Lithuanian landlady's vigorous fumigation program, and there was even room to dance around when the mood struck. All in all, it was quite a satisfactory dwelling.

It had the additional advantage of being very close to the button lady, an ancient creature who had a storefront down the street. The button lady fascinated me, though I was intimidated by her severity. Her face was deeply wrinkled, her eyes were sharp and fierce, her body thin and dried out. She was a woman of few words; one sensed that she had her reasons. She always wore a babushka and old-fashioned clothes that I found very appealing. Her button store had no name or hours of operation. It opened whenever she got to it. Inside, the place was dim and dusty, filled with tall rows of boxes, each meticulously labeled. There was barely room to move between the rows. You couldn't really browse there. You had to tell the old woman something about what you were looking for and then she would pull out a few boxes. The way she did it made you realize she knew precisely where that vast storehouse of old buttons were placed. She loved those buttons. When she held a handful and told you about them, that was the only time you'd see the light in her eyes. They were unique and marvelous, the buttons I got from her. I wish I still had them but like my grandmother's wonderful silk comforter, and the beautiful clothes my mother knitted, they are gone, carelessly dropped along the way like objects left behind at an oasis. So many objects left along the way. The clothing one wore, the furniture one had, the books and music, photographs of events and places, all of such importance at the time. I think that if I saw some of those things again I might not even remember them.

Many of the places I inhabited were so like each other that I can sweep them neatly into a pile and apply one description to them all: worn out walkups in decrepit lower East side tenements, infested with cockroaches. One on Sixth Street, another on Seventh, another on Eleventh, some on streets that I have forgotten. I remember one room clearly because of a color. In a brave attempt to imbue the place with a more poetic ambiance, I painted the walls a lovely cornflower blue. It was a happy improvement, but not long lasting, from my perspective anyway because I moved out a month after I finished painting that gorgeous blue on those bumpy old walls.

Jazz, and especially the excruciating screams of Ornette Coleman's sax, described my sentiments perfectly. With its smoky sensuality, impossibly lyric tenderness, and raw emotional intensity, jazz was something that made sense to me when a great deal about my life made none at all. I was troubled by the big questions. Who am I? What am I supposed to be doing with my life? Why do I feel so alone? Jazz made sense. It gave me a rest from my ongoing inner turmoil. That's why I made regular visits to the Five Spot, where every night black musicians like Miles Davis, Ornette Coleman, Horace Silver and Art Farmer played until 2 AM. It felt good to sit there listening to that music, wearing dark sunglasses in the dark room with the cool remove of the Beat attitude, drinking beer, and watching the black men play. Men absorbed a great deal of my interest in those days, and of all men, I thought black men were the most desirable. If you believed in civil rights and racial equality, which I did, hanging out with black men was one way to tell the world. Black men also had the allure of the forbidden. Hanging out with black men was sure to provoke the narrow-minded bourgeoisie, always an amusing occupation to me at that age. Not the least consideration was the popular myth that black men were wonderful lovers whose significant physical attributes left men of other races dangling, so to speak. I wasn't gullible enough to believe this blindly. I had to learn more about it from personal experience, and I did. I have nothing else to report at the moment. You must do your own research.

My passions in addition to sex were poetry and literature. Two of my closest friends were Marilyn Hacker and Samuel "Chip" Delany, both of whom achieved considerable renown as writers. I met Marilyn in Mme. Balakian's French literature class and we quickly became friends. Marilyn was a precocious 16-year old native New Yorker whose poetic voice was already impressive, a young woman with a prodigious intellect, tremendous curiosity, and a literary gift that was dazzling even then. And she portrayed a certain humorous world-weariness and sophistication that I found impossibly attractive. Marilyn introduced me to her friend and lover Chip Delany, a young black man who also 16, and just as brilliant. In many ways the two of them seemed like psychic twins--a pair of intellectual prodigies who were scintillating, arch, and emotionally complex. Marilyn speaks of this in her poem The Terrible Children:

> *Blood never etched this congruence of curve;*
> *no tie explains the way symmetric swerve*
> *and flash of sound and movement ape each other,*
> *nor explicates the bent, left-handed grace*
> *their yoked forms sing, striding from place to place.*

Marilyn and Chip were stimulating and uncomfortable campadres. They took off into heady explorations of Sartre's existential philosophy and veered into mathematical theory that left me in the dust feeling like a suburban hick, which

I was. They passionately discussed the work of poets and fiction writers living and dead. I valiantly tried to keep up but I never felt sharp enough or quick enough around them. The most uncomfortable thing about friendship with them was witnessing the painful contortions of their relationship. All of us in that circle played games of sexual ambiguity and betrayal, describing our studied distance from our lovers as sexual freedom, but their relationship outdid anything the rest of us dreamed up.

I also thought that Marilyn very brave because she befriended established poets. Now I realize that she was simply following her natural bent, introducing herself to and learning from others with more experience. She and Chip invited me to accompany them when they visited W.H. Auden, but I never went because I was intimidated, sure that my poetry was not good enough to pass the inspection of the great man. I was so afraid of his scorn that I never took the opportunity to meet him. Now I just sit here and shake my head. I was afraid of what I loved and held back from what I wanted. People say that everything is perfect as it is, and it is, yet sometimes the Muses work in strange ways.

After a year and a half I dropped out of college and found my first job as a magazine editor. Leaving college provoked anxiety and concern. It started to buzz around my head like a swarm of wasps. I really did not know what to do next.

But I went on as people usually do, trying my best to bury my anxiety, distracting myself with my daily activities, the new job, eating steak tartar for breakfast to fix my hangover, listening to jazz, buying clothes, enjoying men and writing poems.

The little group that was our gang--Judy, Marilyn, Chip, Pierre, with his endless sailor seduction stories, and Egyptian Victor who moved across the landscape like a massive ship, his umbrella over his arm no matter what the weather-- we were all playing at one or another literary effect, trying our best to make ourselves up in ways we hoped would appear to be sophisticated, witty, and suitably decadent, like our literary icons Anais Nin, Baudelaire, Rimbaud, Henry Miller, Jean Genet and Lawrence Durrell.

Baudelaire was our hero and *les fleurs du mal,* the flowers of evil, our talisman. Baudelaire, the inventor of literary decadance, believed that existence was purposeless. He argued that vice was natural and virtue unnatural. He championed modern artificiality and encouraged taking pleasure in vice rather than goodness. We found this violent romantic cynicism very easy to espouse. Now everything I thought so dazzling in Baudelaire seems a sorry contortion, a glorification of what I find most corrosive in Western industrial society. I say to that girl I was then, "How could you believe all that, love all that, think that was so wonderful?" But she looks at me the way a young woman can look at a woman in her 70s, especially if they are connected as intimately as she and I, and she tells me in an irritated voice, "I don't even recognize me in you any more. Look at you, a Buddhist with prayer beads. You haven't had a lover in years. You're thick in the middle. You don't even dye your gray hair. I never could have imagined I would become you. Why did you change so much?"

If we continued our conversation, she would have to admit that I've become a lot more comfortable with power, love and authenticity than she was in those days. But we're not getting into an extended heart-to-heart at the moment. Right now, I want to comfort her. "Don't worry dear girl," I whisper to her, "I am not going to leave you or forget you. You are part of me."

Writer Joan Didion once said, "We are well advised to keep on nodding terms with the people we used to be, whether we find them attractive company or not." But I don't want just want to be on nodding terms, even though there are considerable expanses of my past and previous personas that I find quite difficult and unfortunate. When I look back at the road I've traveled and regard the traveler, I feel the kind of tenderness one feels for a child who is sad or confused. Oh my word, I think to myself. The ways in which the flower of my being tried to unfold! As I age, as I look back, I want to heal the past, to brush everything with pollen, with dew, with light, to acknowledge and love the earlier me and let her rest her weary head on my lap and be at peace.

I am walking with Marilyn Hacker into the Bronx building where her mother lives alone, her husband having died several years before. I can see Marilyn's thick glasses, her beautiful big brown eyes, her loose long brown hair, her peasant blouse and skirt, her sturdy legs, her sandals. But I cannot see myself. I cannot remember what I looked like, how my hair was cut, or what I was wearing. It's as if I am no longer there, or as if I wasn't ever really there at all, though of course I was. Her mother greets us, small and nervous. She seems lonely. We drink something cold. It feels that nothing really happens there in that airless place of endless muted grieving. Everything in the apartment, from lampshades to couches, is covered with plastic, as if waiting for a season of change, when protective wraps can be taken off again and life can finally resume. Now I am more fully acquainted with this form of muffled purgatory, but at the time, I had little compassion for the plight of Marilyn's mother, a woman who was grieving her losses alone.

I still think of the others, too. Dear blond Pierre, the sorrow of his childhood never completely hidden in his arch smiles, his fierce and hopeless searches for love in the barrows of anonymous sex. Victor I never got near.

The expression in his heavy-lidded eyes was too forbidding. Now my memory of all of them, even who I was then myself, is as unreal as flickering images on moving film. There are only fragments left, conversations about Ouspensky and the fourth dimension, stanzas of poetry Marilyn was writing, snatches of songs, the frightened eyes of the fragile genius mathematician Bartholomew. As Dante wrote so long ago:

> *O vain and worldly cares of*
> *mortal man how fruitless are the*
> *syllogisms that make thee beat*
> *thy wings in downward flight.*

I had my own personal version of Purgatorio unfolding then. It was driven by my desire for recognition, a passion that has been a burden to me for most of my life. A self-created burden, a difficult knot of my own fashioning. I longed to create great art. I lusted after Senor Fame. I thought that the elevating and transformative experience of creating great art would redeem the meanness of my personal history, or the meanness of how I experienced it. It makes me tired to think of the way that the craving for fame flashed through me over and over. It is tempting to dismiss that entire struggle now that it's subsided. But that struggle is part of what brought me to this place. I wanted to be famous. I wanted to create great art that would move and heal myself and others. I have to say I'm grateful that I escaped the notice of Senor Fame and hung out instead with Orestes Obscurity, whose virtues are not well recognized or understood. I think I was lucky to have had the opportunity to unfold more quietly.

One day Marilyn and I decided that we wanted to score some opium, a drug we had never tried. That's how I met my first husband. We headed for Washington Square Park. The word on the street was that a particular man might be able to get some for us. When we found him sitting in the park and proposed the venture, he said that he would try. If I had been there with everything I know now, I would have told that girl, the earlier me, to watch out. I don't know if she would have listened to me though. She was burning, reckless and laced with despair. It turned out that he couldn't get us any opium. That could have been the end of that. I could have left and never seen him again. But I was drawn to him. He was stocky, strong, with dark curly hair and heavy-lidded eyes like the eyes you see in Byzantine mosaics and frescos. He had a tattoo on his left arm, from a prisoner of war camp in Korea. His face was boldly drawn--eyes emphasized by heavy eyebrows, big Italianate nose, full mouth. He was 13 years older than I was and had an air of gangster menace that I found fascinating. He squinted as he spoke, fixing his gaze on some invisible object in the midst of space, as if his vision itself had teeth. His nostrils flared, his mouth turned down into a frightening scimitar-like curve. He looked down his nose as if he were speaking from a powerfully great height, although he was only 5'7" tall. Even the way he picked his teeth was a little intimidating. He was a rough item. There was no doubt about it. He could be quite charming, too. His smile was dazzling, his eyes liquid and inviting. He told dramatic stories of intrigue and confrontation. He also exuded an animal sexuality. His name was Michael, which is the name of an archangel.

Now dear reader, perhaps you already know that there are rooms whose keys we hide from ourselves, fearing to unlock what is in them. There are things we do not know and things that are so charged that whenever they pass through our head, we fall into a stupor, a whole long history of lifetimes behind us whose lessons we have not yet learned or have forgotten all over again, things we are magnetized to, for good or ill, out of habits and beliefs we sometimes don't even know we have. It was like that with me as I fell in love with Michael M. in the lull between the Korean War and the Vietnam War. I enjoyed his intelligence, fierce protectiveness and wild imagination. I found his jealousy charming. He was a good lover. We were like a gangster and his moll, an intellectual Athena and a rough Hercules, a mesmerized maiden and a rapt Svengali.

My friends thought it amusing; they were certain that it wouldn't last long. But Michael M. and I married six months after we met in a judge's office in downtown Manhattan. By then I knew he was a heroin addict. It was the Ides of March. I wore a green dress the color of pea soup and a matching pillbox hat. Two of my friends, a playwright and his girlfriend, were witnesses. They let me know that they did not endorse our union just because they were taking part in the ceremony and left immediately after it was over. "I knew it would come to no good when I saw the color of the dress you were wearing," one of them confided years later. And now that I think of it, it was rather like the color of the walls my mother painted in one of our flats, a color I always thought displayed the tones of our existential distress.

My parents were not happy about my marriage. No one from either of our families attended our wedding. But I believed that finally I had someone who loved me, who would care for me and protect me. I did not consider his heroin habit of much importance. As I live and breathe. What was I thinking? About six months after our wedding, my new husband stole an income tax refund check that he found in our mailbox. The check was addressed to the previous tenant of our apartment, a black actor whose name I still see in New York Times theater reviews. Forging the actor's signature, my bridegroom cashed the check. I didn't know anything about it until the police came to our door to arrest him. I could have left him then.

But I didn't. I was full of sacrificial ideas about marriage from my Catholic upbringing and my own parents' marriage. In that model, it was essential to be loyal in the face of obstacles, no matter how strange or difficult they might be. So I kept pouring myself into it, as if by sheer energy and commitment I could right everything. I was dutiful. I even baked things and brought them down to The Tombs when I visited during the months he was in jail. I also developed a plan for the time when Michael M. was to be released. This was a plan that had already been tried by countless women, usually with bad results, but of course I didn't know that. I planned to get pregnant, reasoning that if he became a father Michael M. would not be tempted to use heroin again. Instead, he would live into his unlived potentials and finish writing the play he was working on. I was determined to help him become the person I knew he really was deep inside. I also had come to realize how much I wanted a child, someone to care for, someone whose existence would give my own life direction and meaning. I never bothered to tell Michael M. It was my little secret. I conceived Danielle the week that he returned home from jail. When the doctor confirmed my pregnancy Michael M. seemed delighted. But it was not long before he was scuttling out of the house late at night to score heroin, returning even later very stoned. Angry, disappointed and anxious for his safety, I dimly realized that my clever plan to transform him wasn't working.

During the 5 years we were married, we were regular participants in Sunday afternoon dinners at various relative's apartments. Almost everyone, men and women, was short and plump, except for Carmine. The wives were great cooks. Those meals were earthly ambrosia. We ate elaborately, Sunday afternoons passing by in gustatory stupefaction as course after course came out of the kitchen. The hard work of consuming everything was lightened with stories, wine, and Coca Cola, that staple digestif of New York Italo-American meals. Over the course of a year of gatherings and holidays, we consumed goose, suckling pig, meatballs, long pieces of flank steak spread with a delicious filling, rolled up, tied in a little bundle, and simmered and breaded brains (Delicious, given to me the first time without a hint of its origin. "No. Just eat a piece first and tell me what you think," Aunt Rose said, smiling mischievously. Do you like it? I did, even when I discovered what it was.) Of course, we had the obligatory gravy, stuff more generally known as tomato sauce, whose preparation was always a matter of much heated discussion.

Started in a big pot in the morning it simmered for hours until the aroma of the tomatoes and whatever meats or vegetables had been added to them suffused the entire apartment. Then it was served with whatever form of pasta, vegetables and adornments the cook chose. Beautifully arranged bowls of fruit and plates of cheese were brought out as we wound down. I'm sure we had desserts, but except for the Easter pie, I no longer recall any of them. The generosity and gaiety of these meals was a revelation to me because I was so habituated to the stingy solemn feeling that permeated gatherings with my mother's side of the family. In contrast to that, any Sunday meal among my in-laws was served up with gusto and graciousness. I offer up these sumptuous repasts du temps perdu as a cameo of what I sought in my marriage to Michael M.--the pleasures of tradition and an experience of trustworthy family connection and love.

Some of the in-laws were colorful, like wisecracking Carmine -- short, quick and handsome. We never called him uncle, just Carmine. Uncle Louis, whose business at the Fulton Fish Market required that he go in and out of a walk-in freezer many times during the day, said that he needed to use brandy to keep warm. There was something furtive and cagey about Louis, but I never learned the details. I just knew him as a magnanimous host who maintained an extravagant display of liqueurs, a splendid arrangement of glass bottles variously shaped, some strangely tall and thin, one a short, thick triangle, some plump and round, and a few sturdy, thick-walled rectangles. On the Sunday I am thinking of, the whole arrangement sparkled in the sun that came in through the window, shining light through the green, gold, pale yellow, milky white, and amber colored liqueurs.

Most of the men in the family were working class stiffs, but Carmine was a cat burglar. He had recently been released from jail after a long time inside. He was found climbing up the wall of the building, or inside the apartment of, or on his way back out of the apartment of the people whose jewels he intended to steal, or stole. When Carmine went to jail, his beautiful wife Violet ran off with Carmine's hand-tailored silk suits and also his best friend. Bitterly, Carmine determined that he would never marry another beautiful woman. So he married a plain one, a slack-bodied 40-year old Irish-English virgin who was in addition not very smart. But in the realm of sex, she was making up for lost time. "God, I hope that woman doesn't kill me," he would sigh, worn out from their prolonged connubial encounters. As I write this, I can hear my mother saying in a voice tinged with bitterness, "Well, you made your bed, now lie in it." My mother certainly lived that way for years herself. So did Carmine the cat burglar, and so did I.

My marriage was tormented but I loved being pregnant. As the baby made herself known inside me with little kicks,

I felt as if I had a place within the pulse of generations. I was determined to give my coming child a healthy nine months in the womb. I stopped smoking cigarettes, used no drugs, ate well and took long enjoyable walks through the city. Still, things happened that were not exactly salubrious. Like the day my husband took me with him to visit the writer Alex Trocchi, who was a heroin addict. His wife, who brought home the bacon through prostitution, and their darling 3-year old son were also at home. As we sat together in their dismal apartment, the little boy began imitating his father shooting up. Watching that child pretend to tie a belt around his arm so that his veins would stand out better, I became dizzy and nearly passed out. It was my most visceral confrontation thus far with the matter at hand, illuminating the decision I would have to make at some point. Would I stay and raise our child in the midst of the drama of addiction, or would I leave in favor of other vistas?

We were at my mother-in-law Jennie's apartment when I went into labor. It was the day after Valentine's Day and we had just finished one of her immense Sunday meals. When she realized that I was in labor, Jennie started shouting at me across the dining room table. "Don't you want to kill him?" she yelled. "Why?" I was able to ask after the pain had passed. "Why? She's asking why." Jennie looked around at the other family members, an expression of disbelief on her face. "Because he did this to you," she explained. "Go ahead," she told me. "Curse him! Curse him!" She couldn't believe it when I told her I didn't feel like cursing him. As far as I was concerned, my husband was not the one who held the power in the situation. It was my journey. I was surprised that my mother-in-law didn't understand that. I was delighted to be in labor. I was looking forward to seeing my baby. But my hymn to fertility, much as it resounded within me all those nine months, finally arrived at a crossroad, and the violins paused with their last notes suspended in the air.

From the warm dining room filled with familiar chatter and smells I had to be delivered to the hospital. Everyone patted me and wished me luck. But the upshot of it was, they all disappeared and I was left lying by myself on a stretcher in a long hallway. The corridor was empty, except for echoes of footsteps that sounded far away. I felt terribly alone, betrayed into the hands of strangers. But that makes no sense, I admonished myself. Everyone has to do it this way. This is the way it is. The bereft, raw feelings were familiar. That's the way it had been with me for years. I was used to toughing it out, to nobody being there to comfort or support me. Even so, I found myself wishing for company, someone who loved me enough to be there. If there was someone, wouldn't they be with me? I would just have to do it myself, as usual.

Not so much a person as an object of hospital business, I was wheeled into a room at last. A nurse gave me a tranquilizing injection and an enema. There was no warmth to the woman whatsoever. Was I just another annoyance in her annoyingly busy day? It felt that way. "You can use that bathroom over there," the nurse told me curtly as she left, pointing to an open doorway across the empty room. My stretcher was the only piece of furniture in the empty room. The open doorway of the bathroom seemed far away. The contractions were coming on stronger. Although the injection made me feel drowsy and uncoordinated, the enema demanded that I get to the bathroom soon. So I eased myself off the stretcher and stood up. What if I fall? Why don't they take care of me? I felt like sobbing, but I forced myself to focus. When I started to walk to the bathroom, I realized that the entire floor of the room was covered with about an inch of broken plaster. They had actually dumped me in a room full of rubble and left me like the victim of a war. Perhaps I was a victim of a war, and this rubble was there to tell me more about it. In one country, far away, there was a dream of love, there was a life full of love, love that was easy, natural, reliable. But I did not live in that country. I lived in the country of my marriage, and that country was full of the rubble of my abandonment.

I climbed back onto the stretcher and lay there exhausted. Finally my doctor arrived. Here at last was someone

I could rely upon and trust, my benevolent old doctor with the sparkly eyes and funny sense of humor. I was wheeled into another room. I had never felt so drugged. Suddenly I had an impulse to flee. The nurses were taking my feet and thrusting them into cold metal stirrups, pushing my legs wide apart as they did it. Why was I being strapped down and pushed open like a piece of meat? They had no right to treat me this way! I had to remain awake. I just didn't trust them. And I wanted to be awake for the birth. My doctor would surely understand why I wanted that. Hadn't they drugged me enough already? I looked up and asked the doctor not to give me any anesthetic. "Oh, you need it," he insisted. "You won't be able to stand the pain." "I've handled the pain so far," I countered. "I want to be awake." For a moment, he looked truly surprised. Then he grinned and motioned to the anesthesiologist, who placed a funnel firmly over my face. I could have killed that doctor if I had the power to do so, but fortunately I didn't. I smelled the sweet smell of the ether and I went spinning down, down, down into a luminous white tunnel.

Right up until the moment that the doctor overrode my wishes about using the ether, I had been feeling angry, afraid and bereft, a poor woman who had to go it alone. I forgot that I was not really alone at all, that none of us is ever alone, no matter what circumstances we find ourselves in. I don't know if I actually understood that then. I suspect I did not.

All that was left behind as I drifted off into etheric realms, floating above my body. I looked down I saw myself lying on the gurney. Then, when I returned into my body, I found that the air around me was trembling with radiance. The details of the delivery room had faded back. I was surrounded by a circle of tall winged beings. Neither male nor female, they were indescribably beautiful, transparent and bright with bodies composed of rainbow light. They were unconfined by physical bodies or the demands and habits of the earth plane. To experience them shimmering so near me expanded me far beyond the boundaries of my usual mindset. I hadn't felt so safe and at home in a very long time. They hovered around me, fanning me with their exquisite wings and saturating me with their limitless love while my body bore down and I brought my daughter Danielle to birth.

How long were they with me? I have no idea. Ordinary time had no meaning there. But strange as it may seem, I became frightened of them. Their blazing beauty was so big. I might disappear forever, drowned in their light. I wondered whether I was dying or if had already died. Had they come to take me away? As doubt and fear ran through me, the winged beings faded until they were just dim, small images in the room. Oh, would they leave me? That prospect filled me with a terrible grief. Even though I was afraid of their splendor and their depth, I yearned for them.

Inwardly I called to them, begging them to return. They began to brighten. Their radiance bathed me as they drew closer. They had such beautiful eyes, eyes that seemed ageless, wise and full of love. Had they always been near me?

One in particular came very near. He bent over me and we talked. Our communication was telepathic. I don't pretend to understand what happened next. "We have come to ask you if you would like to take part in a planetary experiment," the winged being said.

It seemed to take a long time for the words to arrive one by one in my mind, and a long time for me to understand them. Even so, I didn't really understand. I finally understood the words, but I didn't understand why the question was being posed. "Why are you choosing me?" I finally asked, groping for the words in my mind. Language seemed so difficult in the midst of their brightness. "That's not the important part," the winged being responded. "Just tell us if you want to do it. Do you want to exchange the child of your birth for another child from far away in order to further world peace?"

Did angels arrange this sort of thing? What a strange proposition it was. But however odd it seemed, why should I refuse? Did I distrust the messengers or the message? They seemed benevolent and what they asked seemed a noble thing. Of course I wanted to help create world peace.

Was it a test of my trust? Finally I mentally answered the angel who bent over me, "I will exchange the child of my blood for another child from far across the world to help create world peace." There, it was done and the baby was born. They were gone. I opened my eyes.

I still wish those angels had not said any words. I have never understood that part of it. If they had just been still, without all that business about baby-switching for planetary peace, it would be a far less puzzling memory.

Across the room, back in the so-called real world, I saw a nurse holding up a blue baby by its ankles and slapping its back. As I heard the baby's cry, I exhaled with relief.

"It's a girl," the doctor smiled, touching my arm, and I forgot for the moment how angry I had been with him about the anesthesia. "She was born with the umbilical cord wrapped around her neck. That's why she's blue. But she'll be all right," he assured me. "Don't worry. You did fine. You've got a beautiful daughter." Then he was gone.

I saw the baby for a moment. She was so blue, so long and thin. I wanted to hold her, but I was very tired. When I woke up, I had no idea how much time had elapsed. A nurse with gray hair was busy making the next bed with her back to me. "Can you bring my baby to me, please?"

I asked the old nurse. She did not respond but continued making the bed. I grew anxious. Was something wrong?

"Where is my baby?" I asked again, raising my voice. "I want to see my baby!" Still the nurse made no response. Then I began to wonder if my baby was dead. That thought undid me. "My baby, my baby," I wailed loudly. Two other nurses immediately responded. The old nurse, who must have been quite deaf, turned in surprise at the rush of activity. Soon I was holding Danielle. She was pink! She had dark hair, and she was beautiful. What can I say about that moment? To gestate a child within you for nine months, to go through the process of birth, and then to hold in your arms a distinct new being who has come out of your body is something mysterious and wonderful.

That day, Michael M. came to visit. Greeting me happily, he held the baby, cooed over her, then gave her back to me. He sat down in a chair next to the bed. Soon he was nodding out, catching himself with a start, opening his eyes, rubbing his nose. I was mortified and angry. How shameful. *Disgraciada!* as they say in an Italian family. How dare he. The junkie husband shows up stoned to see his daughter for the first time. Why had I ever married him? Why was I caught in this ugly net? I wanted to greet my new daughter with a pristine world, not introduce her to a junkie father and an angry mother on her very first day of life. Yet there it was. I remembered how I had hoped that the baby would change everything, and I cried.

For the next two years, I was living in two worlds. One was the sweet, busy world of the baby and me, and the other was the difficult, scathing world of my husband's anger and addiction. I had never loved anyone as much as I loved Danielle. I loved nursing her, bathing her, holding her, bundling her up and taking her out for walks in the winter mornings. When she laughed out loud for the first time as I lifted her above me while we lay on the bed, I thought I would dissolve from the joy of hearing the sound of her laughter and seeing the delight on her little face.

A baby evokes wonder because it is still close to the angels. Its newness melts us—its skin soft as a flower petal, that sweet breath, those tiny hands and feet—It sometimes appears that the baby is not quite in her body yet but lingers still in luminous realms that have become invisible to us more solid beings. Perhaps that's why being with a baby brings us back to the state of beginners' mind, beginners' eyes, beginners' smile. I felt that way about Danielle. When I looked into her eyes, it was like gazing out into the spacious reaches of the universe, or deep inside the secret wisdom of the uncreated.

My relationship with Michael M. was more problematical. One night after dinner, he locked himself in the bathroom.

I knew that he shot up heroin when he disappeared into the bathroom, although it was a subject we never discussed. That night he was in the bathroom for a very long time. I knocked on the door, quietly at first, so that our landlady, who lived downstairs, wouldn't notice. Getting no answer, I pulled at the door until the little latch gave way. He was sitting on the toilet, and he was an awful shade of blue. His mouth hung open, drool dribbled down from it. His eyes were turned up. The needle was still in his arm. Was he dead? How dare he? I slapped his face several times in a mixture of anger and concern, but he didn't move. I started shaking. I knew had to call the ambulance but I didn't want them to find his paraphernalia and implicate me.

Gingerly, I took the needle from his arm and picked up the other paraphernalia from the floor. Walking into the kitchen, I put it into a plastic freezer container. Then I poured some of the marinara sauce I had made for dinner into the container, put the lid onto it, and stuck it in the freezer. While I was doing it, the maneuver reminded me of something from an Alfred Hitchcock movie but I was too agitated to give it any real appreciation. I called the ambulance. By the time they got my husband strapped down to the stretcher, he was hallucinating. He thought that he was back in Korea and that the paramedics were enemy soldiers taking him prisoner. He fought them with all the strength his stoned condition allowed. They managed to subdue him. When everyone left, it was quiet again. I was still shaking. The baby had slept through the whole thing.

Of course, after that incident the landlady and landlord didn't want us there anymore. We moved to an apartment on the lower East Side. I was in a state of deep confusion. I didn't know what to do with my feelings. I didn't know how to find a solution for my desperate predicament.

One day I got so angry at my husband that I put my fist through a pane of glass in a French door. My lack of control frightened me so much that I decided to commit myself for treatment in an open psychiatric ward. Danielle was 9 months old. I knew I would never hurt her, but I was afraid I might hurt my husband or myself. I needed help and time to think.

Even muffled by Stelazine or Thorazine, I found the experience of the psychiatric ward curiously liberating. For once, no one was pretending that everything was okay. No Queen of Denial mother-in-law was assuring me that her son wasn't a heroin addict, that he had always been a good boy. No husband Pity Me and Love Me was telling me that he was dying of cancer, and that everything would be wonderful if only he lived. As if that cancer fantasy of his was really the problem. I was relieved to be there in a world where nothing whatsoever pretended to be normal or denied what was happening. It was unpredictable, visceral and very poignant.

The thin poetic son of a famous newspaperman walked through the halls playing his flute, a desperately unhappy expression on his face. The obese woman with the tiny, thin husband periodically attacked some poor aide. Then they quenched her anger with electric shock therapy. One pretty, plump woman insisted that she was there only to lose weight. The whimsical gay black man never said anything about why he was there. During my three-month stay I never told anyone why I was there, either.

When my mother-in-law brought Danielle to visit, my little girl looked at me with solemn eyes, as if I was a stranger. That made my heart ache. But I didn't have the strength to go back to my house. The mere thought terrified and exhausted me. After three months in the hospital I returned to my marriage, which was definitely a landslide in progress.

A few months later, I determined to leave. Michael M. was at work. Danielle was in the care of some friends. The coast was clear, or so I thought. I was packing up our clothes when the front door opened and Michael M. charged in. There I was, with the bleeding key in my hand, just like the woman in the story of Bluebeard. The room you are not supposed to enter in this case turns out to be the exit.

"What do you think you're doing?" he shouted. In a state of shock, I said nothing. "You were planning to leave, weren't you?" he asked, grabbing my blouse. How had he figured it out? In the terror of that moment, I began to understand the threat that had kept me with him so long. He had never hurt me because I had never stepped out of line. "You thought you could fool me, didn't you?" he leered, his face pressed against mine. "But you couldn't, could you?" He began to rip my clothes off, hitting me, biting me, kissing me. Then he put his hands around my neck and began to strangle me. "Stay with me," he growled.

Violent moments speed by like comets; we don't know where or how they will finish their flight. In just that way, I wondered if the time of my death had come. I wanted to stay alive to raise my daughter. So I assumed a subservient attitude. In response, he loosened his grip for a moment, surprised. "Okay," I gasped. "Let's try again." I knew I had taken him off guard. It was strange to see how he could be so fixed one moment, and so vagrant the next. But then he was back on me again, his hands around my neck. "I don't trust you. Where's Danielle?" he shouted, throttling me. "I want her. Where is she? Tell me, or I'll kill you."

Desperately afraid, I told him. He spat at me then ran out leaving me shaking. Galvanized by the need to get to Danielle before he did, I threw my clothes on and ran down to the police station a block away. I arrived with a policeman just in time to prevent him from taking Danielle. The police detained him. I finished packing and left for good.

Then it was a life of hiding. He wouldn't let me be. Once he found out where I was, stood on a nearby roof, waving a long curved knife and shouting, "I'm going to kill you. Do you hear me? I'm going to kill you."

When you are being hunted, you have to be very alert. You have to cover your tracks. You have to stay hidden. You have to change jobs, move from place to place, make a whole new life. Your head may be filled with tigers, your dreams may be crowded with dangerous men, and your house and mind may be an uneasy prison. You may fear for your child and yourself. But you have to keep on going. Finally one day I opened the curtains and the sun was shining. Fortuna smiled on me. The fire of that marriage gradually burned to ashes and I started to emerge, a young woman who had been through some kind of Hell.

Only years later, in the reflective theater of memory, where I was able to watch the drama again from a distance, did I begin to understand anything about what I chose when I married him-- a caricature of my parents' anguished marriage, made even more extreme by physical threat. I think my parents might have loved each other more. They seemed to have tender feelings about each other even after they divorced. Each of them would say to me separately, and sadly, "There will never be anyone like your Mother. There will never be anyone like your Father."

You know that song Billie Holliday sings, titled *No Regrets?*
I regret some things, including my first marriage. It's a
regret not so much for myself as for my daughter. I wish
I could go back and choose another father for her. I wish
I could go back and be a better mother to her, my daughter Danielle, who began to drink seriously when she was
14, and who hasn't stopped yet. My beautiful, fast-talking,
high-strung 47-year old daughter who never knew her
father, yet who has been so much like him in ways that do
not benefit her.

For months after fleeing Michael M., I lived in hiding
in various friends' apartments and homes like a rabbit
cowering in its hole out of sight of the hawk, unsure
about whether it was safe to emerge yet. Had the raptor
finally disappeared? Silence. Silence. Months of being left
in peace, though the hypervigilance I felt can't rightly be
called peace. It was a long siege, grieving and hiding while
working and raising a child alone. I hoped that I had finally
eluded him, but I was never quite certain that I had. Months
passed. New Year's Eve arrived. This New Year's Eve, I told
myself firmly, would mark a new chapter in my life. I would
start again.

We like to tell ourselves that, and we do start over, though
it seldom has the breadth and depth of change we wish for.
I felt skittish, excited at the prospect of going out for the

first time in many months. My witty photographer friend Peter offered to be my escort; he appeared with a list of parties we could attend. Our first stop was a loft on the Bowery, the home of a couple introduced as Mort and Kate. Mort's assemblages and paintings hung on the walls, and Mort himself strode around, skinny and wild-eyed, glad-handing everybody. Kate, her full body squeezed into a tight sparkly little dress, was already quite sloshed. Her mascara and eyeliner had begun to drift around outside of their prescribed territory. What a heart, and what heart-ache. You could see it all as soon as you looked into those big, kind, grief-stricken eyes. What a kind, loving drunk. She reminded me of my father.

The big open loft space was full of partygoers, an ornate collection of human beings, all busy smoking pot and cig-arettes, drinking beer and wine, making erotic overtures to one another, gyrating wildly and holding animated conversations. I thought I had died and gone to heaven. Was it possible that I might be coming back to take my place among the city's artists, certainly the most real of all possible people? I was prone to exaggerate the qualities of both the living and the dead in those days.

That was the evening I met Jerome. I heard his laughter before I saw him on the other side of the big room. He was a tall, bear-like man with light brown hair and a round face decorated by a short beard. His twinkly blue eyes were framed by wire-rimmed glasses. I liked his looks immediately. In spite of his size he had an elfin quality. I liked the sound of his laughter.

I couldn't have told you I hoped for a love bright enough to burn away and transform the isolation and bitterness of my life because I could barely admit it to myself. My way of dealing with men and romance had been to play the part of an amazon seducer, a well-defended woman who extolled the virtues of sex without love. I did everything I could to protect myself against the real intimacies of love because they terrified me. Loving men demanded too much vulnerability. It was unreliable, dangerous and painful.

But by the time I met Jerome, I was awfully weary of wearing so much armor and being so emotionally undernourished. I was seriously parched, ready for some convincing proof of love's nourishing and healing potentials.

The first thing I thought about Jerome was that he looked very happy. I had not had much contact with very happy men up until then, so that in itself was attractive. He noticed me across the room and came over to meet me. We danced, laughed, and talked together for much of the evening. I found him delightful and started to fall in love with him right then and there. It surprised me. But why should I have been surprised? I was longing for a redeeming love.

We became inseparable. He wooed me by singing plaintive Irish songs, fearlessly intoning arias from operas and playfully sharing Beatles tunes. I had never met a man with such expansive, passionate regard for art and life. He loved music and poetry. Each time he launched into poems like The Love Song of J. Alfred Prufrock or Sailing to Byzantium I fell in love with him all over again.

For the first time in my life, I felt cherished by a man. I am still grateful for the sweet mantle he placed on me. The difficulties I had just endured made our encounter even more poignant. What a miracle, I thought to myself as the days went by, seeing how Jerome and Danielle enjoyed each other's company. Jerome paid more attention to Danielle than her father ever had. Soon Danielle and I were spending most of our time at his cozy wood-paneled Chelsea apartment, roasting marshmallows in front of the fireplace, telling stories, laughing, dancing, drawing pictures.

Our romance was quite wonderful. But it had its share of gargoyles and weeping, too because Jerome had a dark secret. He was impotent. I didn't want it to matter, and most of the time, it didn't, not from my perspective anyway. He gave me a lot of pleasure. But his sexual difficulty, which he refused to talk about, tormented him.

I'm not sure that our romance would have survived the challenges posed by his impotence and my own unhealed sorrows, not without help. As it turned out, we didn't have the opportunity to test ourselves in that way.

Three weeks after we met, Jerome caught a cold. But how important is a cold when you are in love and a new year has begun? We continued to go to parties and movies and to hang out at Orient Espresso, the coffee shop Jerome ran with his partner Wally. As Jerome's health worsened, his mood changed dramatically. He became agitated and anxious. This was not the Jerome I knew, or thought I knew. I didn't understand how a simple cold could propel such a radical transformation. Everything irritated and disturbed him. Wearily, he told me that he needed a quiet place where he could rest and recover. So he arranged for all three of us to stay with his friends Lex and Sheila Hixon, whose spacious home overlooked the Palisades of the Hudson River.

Not long after we greeted our host and hostess, Jerome was in bed, fast asleep. I put Danielle to bed soon after, assuring myself that things would be better in the morning. I was not sleepy. The events of the past few days had charged me with questions. Why had he changed so dramatically when he caught the cold? Was there a hidden side to him? If it wasn't that, what was it? Something felt terribly wrong. It was painful and confusing. I just wanted my joyful, spontaneous friend back. Hadn't I lived under a large rock long enough? With these thoughts in my mind,

I walked quietly through the big house, recalling my first meeting with Jerome, and thinking of everything that had happened in the short time that we had been together.

One room caught my attention. And this moment deserves notice because it was one of those apparently minuscule events whose influence continues through the years. The room was large and pleasant, square in shape, with high ceilings and tall windows. It contained no furniture, except for a few meditation cushions placed in a line on the carpet. Even standing at the doorway, the implications of the room made me uneasy. Finally, with what I remember as great caution, even fear, I took several steps into the room.

On a mantle I saw photographs of people whom I thought must be spiritual teachers. They were certainly not ordinary people. It was not only their unusual clothing or lack of clothing that distinguished them. It was their eyes and the expressions on their faces. The face of one had a kind of unearthly radiance and joy. The eyes of another had a penetrating quality, as if he saw through everything that met his gaze. There were one or two others, but I cannot remember them. The faces in those photographs stirred and provoked me. At that time, I knew no one who had a spiritual teacher or who placed photographs of spiritual teachers on the mantle as if it were an altar, no one who kept a room empty of the furniture of everyday life as a way of consecrating it to spiritual practice.

It had been many years since I last sat next to my secret friend the mountain hermit in the brilliant sun and snow and those years had been filled with the labyrinthine pathways and struggles of earthly life. Perhaps there was still a world where everything was pristine and resonant with light. But I did not remember it. I had not thought about it for many years (except for my meeting with the angels when Danielle was born.) Yet something about the room called my deeper memory as I stood there restlessly looking at the photographs and the row of meditation cushions. I sensed the room's invitation. I finally did sit down on one of the meditation cushions, but I was restless and worried. I couldn't bring myself to stay for more than a few moments. Brief as it was, I note that interlude as a way station.

The next morning Jerome worsened; Lex arranged for him to be admitted to the VA Hospital. A feeling I had the day before, of Jerome being swept away from me on a big river, grew stronger. But now I was with him on that river too, knowing less and less about the waters that swept us on. The hospital was big, gray, mechanical and cold. Jerome was pale and exhausted. How could we have wound up there in such a shrouded, desolate prison when just a few days before, we were dancing and singing in the winter sun without a care in the world? I didn't want to give him up to that hellish place. But I had no say in the matter.

A few hours after we arrived at the hospital, he began to hallucinate. In the beginning, his visions were about me. He saw harm in my way. Violent men wanted to kill me. He saw them lying in wait for me, and he could do nothing to protect me. Clutching my arm, he begged me to assure him that I would be careful. Then he cried hysterically, begging me to forgive him for leaving me when I was so vulnerable.

Was he leaving me? As it turned out, he was. Jerome couldn't do anything to protect me from the violent men he saw in his visions; I was just as afflicted. I had no idea what illness he was suffering with. The doctors wouldn't tell me anything about his condition because I was not legally related. I couldn't do anything to save him from his dark visions or the unwholesome atmosphere of that surreal hospital. Sitting next to his bed on the second day, I began to realize how little I knew about the actual details of his life. I had no idea what his illness was or what qualified him to be treated at the VA Hospital. I didn't know why he was hallucinating. And then, two days later, Jerome died. I was not there. Nobody was. He died alone. He died. And that was it. I never saw him again.

That was it. That was it. Then I was walking back and forth in his wood-paneled apartment. Back and forth, back and forth. How could it be that he was gone, gone, without a trace!

Cruel, unbelievable, untrue. Dead. Impossible. But they said it was so. It must be so then. I wanted to be alone with him, to say goodby. But I had no legal hold. I could not wash his body or dress it for his burial. I was just a woman who loved him deeply for a brief, bittersweet time. As his body was sent back to his mother in southern California, I remained in New York in the winter wind, with leaves blowing up around my head, walking, walking, walking as if in walking I could breathe him in until he lived in me again. I was left there at the edge of the river with an aching heart and a myriad questions.

Why had his life ended when he was only thirty-three? Why hadn't he told me that he once had rheumatic fever? Why had he pushed himself to the edge that separates health from illness, why had he catapulted into death? Was it because he could not bear loving under the burden of his impotence? Of course there was the awful question-- was our love the cause of his death? And then, once those questions hung in the air, there was left only the final wail-- why had he left Danielle and me alone? Why?

In the turmoil following his death, I had to look for a new place to live. Jerome and I had been planning to find a new place together and both of our apartments had already been rented to new tenants. I hastily chose a two-bedroom place in Spanish Harlem, where Danielle and I lived for the next two years. I don't know how I accomplished the move. Every day was a fog of grieving. I don't recall who helped me move. I don't know what I did with Jerome's things, or if it was I who packed them. Maybe Jerome's business partner Wally packed them up and sent them to Jerome's mother.

I don't remember the wake we held. I don't remember where it was, what we did, or if I was even there. I don't think I was. I have blotted it out entirely. I still have a copy of the memorial poem that Lex Hixon wrote. Other than that, I have only one token to remember Jerome by, a small metal object engraved with the word POETRY. As far as mementos go, it says everything. A song from a Shakespeare play that he liked to sing to me began to seem prophetic. I wondered whether somewhere inside himself he knew how our brief love would end.

> *"Sing unto my roundalay*
> *drop a briny tear with me*
> *dance no more at holy day*
> *like a running river be.*
>
> *my love is dead,*
> *gone to his death bed*
> *all under the willow tree."*

I had never felt the weight of such love or such grief. I wanted to live the rest of my life in silence beneath a black veil. It seemed that joy would dishonor the magnitude of his passing. Yet his wholeheartedness and generosity were so vivid for me. I realized then that in order to keep the gifts he had given me alive, I would have to embody them myself. He would not have wanted me to consign myself to grieving shadows. He would have wanted me to continue to dance in the fountains of poetry on the streets of ordinary life. Knowing that helped me as I grieved his loss. I took up the cup of life again, changed profoundly by our brief love.

I began to work as an assistant to moviemaker Conrad Rooks. A tall, slender blond man in his 30s, Rooks was heir to a fortune. I no longer remember the details of his inheritance. His wife, a beautiful dark-haired woman, was said to be a Russian princess. I never questioned this assertion from a historical perspective at that time, but now I wonder, could she really have been a Russian princess?

Rooks had just produced a film called Chappaqua, which still has a small cult following. In Chappaqua, a psychedelic foray into the world of consciousness expansion and spirituality, Rooks rounded up everyone whose presence might add to the artistic and spiritual flavor-- William Burroughs, Alan Ginsberg, some Tibetan lamas, Indian sadhus, various avant garde artists, and a bevy of Andy Warhol cohorts, who were much sought after in those days.

Rooks' office was on the ground floor of his townhouse. That place was, from my perspective, quite elegant. There while I sat typing letters and answering the phone, as keenly aware of my menial status as any clerk in a Dickens novel, Rooks entertained some of the brightest stars in the art world with the casual familiarity that wealthy people command so easily. Occasionally the beautiful dark-haired princess appeared to talk something over with him. For all their beauty and wealth, they had an edgy, dissatisfied quality. I noticed it but never thought too much about it, because few people I knew were happy or satisfied.

Rooks' life seemed terribly glamorous to me. When Chappaqua was released, he hosted a huge party at an uptown club. Hundreds of people pulsed like a colony of anemones on the dance floor while the band produced a mighty sea of sound. There was plenty of food and drink. People were happy to be there. And Rooks and his Russian princess, at the center of attention, seemed happy, too.

I was just a hired hand. The thought made me glum. If only I had money and connections like Rooks, who knows what great things I could do as an artist. While I was engrossed in these habitual reveries, a man dressed in a long saffron robe walked into the room, moving slowly and gracefully. His long silver-gray hair spread out over his shoulders, and his long silver-gray beard flowed down over the front of his saffron colored robe. I don't think he looked directly at me as he passed, but I remember his dark peaceful eyes. I had never seen eyes like those eyes on a living person. The most remarkable thing about him was a golden light that seemed to radiate from his entire body.

When I saw that light, I wondered if I had perhaps smoked too much marijuana. The room seemed curiously still to me, even with the band playing. Everything was moving very slowly. Finally I managed to pull myself from timelessness to ask a nearby acquaintance, "Who is that?"

"That's Swami Satchidananda," the person replied. It seemed surreal to see such a being, someone like the pictures of spiritual teachers that I had glimpsed on Lex Hixon's mantle, in the midst of that celebratory and world-weary gathering. When Swami Satchidananda finished his slow, luminous passage through the room and disappeared from sight, the party seemed very dark and smoky indeed. But the memory of the golden light he shed remained.

As Aleksandr Solzhenitsyn wrote, "Some things lead us into a realm beyond words . . . to revelations unattainable by reason. It is like that small mirror in fairy tales -- you glance in it and what you see is not yourself; for an instant you glimpse the Inaccessible, where no magic carpet can take you. And the soul cries out for it."

It was like when I saw Swami Satchidananda. The difference between him and the rest of the people at the party was palpable. Seeing him walk through the frenetic smoky nightclub with his saffron robes, silver hair, beatific, aware expression and golden light brought up so much in me. He was without a doubt someone who could be described as a holy person.

But in my mind, he was too far above me, too rarified; he came from another universe than the one I inhabited. I was uncouth, too rude and rough to relate to a being like that. So his appearance scathed me, reminding me of how embroiled and confused I was. There it is—I saw a spiritual teacher for the first time in a smoky nightclub. I can't say that after that I began a zealous single-pointed search for a spiritual teacher or path, but I did begin to search in some fashion. I burrowed in the dark, trying to find my way, and my journey was often a secret even to myself.

I left New York a few years later. At first, I had given my heart completely to that city, believing that it was the only possible place to be, that nothing of substance happened outside of its boundaries. I was in love with New York's power, with its shimmering promise of fame and success. But, as often happens in passionate love affairs, I fell out of love with it completely, feeling in the end like an obedient wife who had surrendered her identity to a demanding, distant husband, hoping for his recognition and love, but discovering instead that she must resign herself to a destiny of drab, humdrum years.

It wasn't just the isolation of my life there, the pervasive sense of danger that I felt, or my concern for my daughter's well-being, though those things figured large. I wanted a life that nurtured me more. How had I forgotten streams, trees, meadows, woods, beaches, rivers, seasons, storms, sunrises? Me, the girl who always used to dream of living like an Indian, the one who turned herself into a magic horse and ran with the wind. It was as if I had been asleep for years, and maybe in some way, I had been. Just the thought of being close to nature made me feel very awake again. In fact, I began to yearn for nature as ardently as I had once longed to fall into the massive embrace of New York.

I started to dream of leaving my door unlocked, walking out in the soft night under the stars, surrounded not by the apartments of people who acted as if I did not exist, but by friends with whom I would share meals, laughter and music. I wanted to breathe sweet air, to get up in the morning and run around barefoot in meadows or streams like a kid. I wanted to be part of a family or community. That's how the city died on me. The marvelous scintillating scales of its dragon body dimmed, its terrible eyes lost their power, the blasts of its fiery breath were extinguished, until finally its immense corpse lay there in full daylight in the stinking air of its decay, and all its jewel treasures, music, architecture, poetry, literature, finance, fashion, cuisine, and all the tales of its famous inhabitants, living and dead, just lay there around it like a dangerously fascinating display from another world, saturated with spells and conjuring I no longer wished to serve.

I speak as if I knew something of magic then, but I knew very little, not only of magic, but of myself. Somewhere inside me I hoped that magic existed, but I didn't have any evidence. I didn't know that I had created and slain the dragon of New York with my mind. I didn't know about the creative power of thought, the magical doorways that choice opens, or the splendid magic of coincidence. I had no idea that I was intuitive and so I knew nothing about how intuition can be like a lamp or torch, lighting the way. I didn't know that my hands were healing or that my life was precious.

I didn't know that I was precious, not only as a unique constellation of potentials but also an inherently holy and whole being. I experienced myself as a nobody, a faker who covered the truth of her failure with witty, cynical repartee, a woman obstructed and confused by conflicting emotions and motives. That's why the notion of surrendering my allegiance to New York was frightening. I had defined myself only through proximity to the city's vast brilliance. Who was I without that? What light of my own was there to use? Could I really cut loose the ship of my life and venture forth to taste the air of other places-- unknown, unsophisticated, unremarkable places though they might be?

When I think about this time in my life, I feel considerable tenderness for the unsure, feisty woman I was. I had no idea what I wanted to create. Only my yearning for another, gentler way of life stirred and guided me. I quit my job as a magazine editor and headed for the Pennsylvania countryside, where Danielle and I stayed with various friends in their beautiful old farmhouses. It was relaxing to live without planning for tomorrow. Because I was not only a roving gypsy but also a bit of a raving maenad, I had affairs with a number of men, including a Black Panther, an older Jewish psychodramatist recently divorced, a darling young black guy named Floyd, a dear witty photographer friend, and the habitually philandering husband of a couple I was close to. I drank a lot of Rolling Rock beer, wrote poetry and stories and walked around in the woods and fields, wondering how to unearth some new kind of vision for my life.

One hot summer day I encountered the mystic teachings of Casteneda. I was on my way into Philadelphia to visit

Floyd. Stopped at a red light, I noticed that the truck in front of me had a bumper sticker that said, *"Watch my rear, not hers."* This irritated me considerably. In a vehicular Freudian reflex, I stepped on the gas and hit the truck's rear end. Naturally, the irate driver, as big a bozo as his bumper sticker promised, slowly got out of the cab of his truck and scowling ferociously, made his way toward me. I pulled out the stops, playing the brainless woman for all I was worth, batting my eyes a lot for good measure. I must have rolled over enough to suit him, because he finally let up and drove off. His truck had sustained no damage whatsoever, but I had broken a hole in the radiator of my car in the collision. I pulled over and called Floyd. Floyd was completely good-natured and laid-back about the whole thing. He picked me up, drove me to his apartment and went off to a junkyard to look for another radiator for my car. When I remember how handsome, mellow, funny and kind Floyd was, and what a great lover he was besides, I am glad that I am a woman with a past that includes him.

I turned the fan on full blast in Floyd's very hot apartment. Finding a big pitcher of Kool-Aid in his refrigerator, I poured myself a tall glass. The current issue of Esquire Magazine was lying on a table in the living room. The photograph on its cover, meant to illustrate an excerpt from Carlos Casteneda's first book, depicted a beautiful naked man diving down over a long waterfall. I had just heard a little about Casteneda and I was very curious. Opening the magazine eagerly, I began to read. Soon I was spellbound. After awhile, I wanted to look at the cover photograph of the beautiful naked man again. As I studied the photograph and thought about what I had read, I glanced at my hands, which seemed strangely translucent and full of rainbows. Little rainbows streamed out of each pore. The lines on my nails radiated rainbows. I sighed, and closing my eyes, I thought to myself, "That Casteneda really is an incredibly powerful writer." The rainbows were still there when I opened my eyes again. I went back to the magazine and finished the book excerpt. As time went on that hot afternoon, and rainbows were succeeded by other interesting visual phenomena, I realized that the Kool-Aid in Floyd's refrigerator must have had acid in it. That's how I was introduced to Casteneda's adventures. It still seems an apt way to have met them.

A few weeks later, I received the gift of a powder blue Plymouth Valiant from my married lover. It was a great getaway car, not big on style but steady on the road. I painted the word POETRY in black paint on the door on the driver's side. Around my neck, I wore a talisman from my dead love Jerome, engraved with that same word-- Poetry. I don't know what anyone else thought reading the word Poetry on the side of my blue car, but I felt comfortable when I saw it there, because poetry had been my most reliable companion. Poetry inspired me, releasing me from my habitual constraints, the worry about how I appeared to others and the concern over whether I had what I imagined it takes, and reading Poetry there like a memo I had written to myself allowed me to relax into a more spacious way of being.

So fortified, I packed some clothes and one summer day in 1971, or somewhere thereabouts, my Danielle and I set out for California. I keenly recall the feeling of hopefulness and freedom that accompanied my preparations and the buoyant quality as we left, Danielle sitting next to me as we drove out across Pennsylvania in the brilliant sun of summer. What an exhilarating feeling it was to get into that car and take off, leaving behind every place and person familiar to my first 30 years on Earth. It was the end of my first Saturn return, a major life passage when, according to astrology, a person has the opportunity to come into her own more fully by cutting parental ties and leaving the world of childhood and adolescence behind.

Though I had never heard of the first Saturn return, I had all the signs and symptoms. An urgent pressure was on me to shed the skin of my old life. I wanted to bury for good the sad reminders of my childhood, those years in Manhattan, and the story of my first marriage. When you go to a new place where no one knows you, I told myself, you can become a new person. I could feel the expansiveness of this possibility, even if I had no inkling of the details of my next incarnation.

In those days, there was no better place for a hippie and nature-lover to be than California. It's true that Woodstock happened on the East coast, but everything else took place in California, a territory awash in golden freedoms, paradisiacal magic landscapes, and the excitement of being right in the midst of the cultural hocus-pocus. I had no land to hold me in place, and plenty I wanted to leave behind. I believed that it would be better to be in California, even if the whole place did break off from the mainland and sink into the sea as Atlantis had so long ago. That's what many of my friends predicted was going to happen, though now it appears that their timing was off.

While getting to California fired my imagination, driving across America did not. I was not wild about America. And of course I had my reasons, which started early on. Can the items in this litany be blamed on my country? I don't know whether it's at all reasonable. But that's what I blamed it all on. I imagined living in pervasive peace yet was born in the midst of a terrible war, and that war begot further wars. As a creature open to big dreaming, I imagined living in a beautiful mythic place in Nature. Instead, I lived in the confinement of New Jersey suburbs. I dreamed of ecstatic language, poetry and music as a natural part of everyday life, but found that we were consigned to a terrible banality. As I grew up, wars proliferated, Nature continued to be eclipsed by industrial development, and spirit was just given lip service, ignored or maligned.

Those were the roots of my alienation from America. Why get excited about driving across a country bereft of culture, art and spirit, where truly ugly architecture, mass-produced food, burgeoning pollution, the blue hypnosis of television and various other forms of social ignorance offer continuous reminders of what a sorry state the place was in? Such were my deep ruminations. I felt like an expatriate, but nonetheless, there I was cruising along on Route 70.

No matter what your political or spiritual malaise, when you get behind the wheel to take your first transcontinental road trip, the magnitude and splendor of the land itself rises up in your imagination and takes over, sweeping away, at least temporarily, a great deal of your philosophy. That first day, we drove through the gently rolling green hills of the Pennsylvania and Ohio countryside, then through Indiana and Illinois until we reached the college town of Columbia, Missouri in the heart of Mark Twain country. We spent the night with the wife of a poet friend from Provincetown days.

The next day, under a brilliant blue sky filled with billowing clouds, we drove across the Missouri River as expansive vistas of Kansas cornfields unrolled in the sun. It was an optimistic summer day, with nothing but the vast sweep of fields and sky, and roads leading in every direction. I was tempted by the thought of getting off the beaten track to take the kind of random drive we took during childhood with my father at the wheel. "Let's just take this road," he would smile. "We've never gone here before." But I couldn't convince myself to do it. I was impatient to get to California.

Finally we came upon San Francisco's expansive bay, its bright lights and the exhilarating smell of the ocean. I had made it to the other side. My life was about to change in ways I could never have imagined.

Chapter 3   Whale Medicine:
Into the Deeps

I have a feeling that my boat
has struck, down there in the depths
against a great thing.
And nothing
happens! Nothing...Silence...Waves
--Nothing happens?
Or has everything happened
and are we standing now, quietly, in the new life?
--JUAN RAMON JIMINEZ, TRANSLATED BY ROBERT BLY

A PICTURE IN ONE OF MY childhood storybooks is imprinted indelibly in my memory. The story it illustrated vanished from my mind long ago but the painting is as clear as if I were holding the well-worn book in front of me. The picture shows a seascape at night. Vast water stretches out to the horizon. A dark night sky filled with billowing clouds is lit by a full moon.

From the mood of sea and sky, it seems that a storm is on the way. I loved that moody image; its expansive turbulence set my imagination flying. In fact, some days when I gazed at the picture I did fly. Turning into a big seabird I flew out of the living room into the night of the picture, where beating my wings in the wind, I had a panoramic view of the billowing clouds, bright moon and stormy sea.

From my vantage point high in the sky I had a great view of the one other element in the picture, a sperm whale. The whale was a very important element, in fact the whale was the main character in the drama. The whale was swimming in the midst of the wild darkness, its enormous bulk lit by the full moon. What an impossibly strange and fascinating creature that whale seemed to me. Its gigantic body and strange square-shaped head puzzled me deeply. After months of studying that picture, I concluded that the sperm whale was not really beautiful, not the way an eagle or a wolf or a deer were beautiful. Instead it was outlandish, almost like a creature from another world. Perhaps that's what I found so compelling. I wondered what would it feel like to be that whale, to plunge deep into the sea and then hurl up out of the water the way the sperm whale did in the next picture, where it had been struck with harpoons. Roaring up out of the ocean, it aroused a massive confusion in the water, throwing tiny boatfuls of whalers into the air with its enormous tail.

I had no use for the harpoons; they appalled me. I didn't like the whalers either, though I felt sad for them as they flew through the air with surprised and frightened expressions on their faces. It was the whale I loved, in all its outlandish bulk and mysterious power. The clouds, the moon, the ocean and the whale were enough for me. Even when I was very young, the whale seemed a creature that embodied some kind of timeless wisdom connected with the secrets of the deeps, the deeps not only of oceans but of the heart and spirit.

If I had been raised in an Indian household, they would have known that I was drawn to the whale medicine and the whale magic. As it happened, it didn't matter at all that I was being raised as a white girl on the reservation of northern New Jersey, that I knew nothing about totem animals, power animals or animal spirit guides. Some people say that you don't have to search for your totem animals, because they find you. That was certainly the way it was with me and the whales.

The next whale I saw was an immense model of a blue whale in the American Museum of Natural History in New York City. My mother, brother and I went on an expedition to the museum one day. It was a journey inspired by my brother's collecting habits. My brother was known as Flip in those days. He had such a penchant for bringing turtles and other creatures home from nearby streams and rivers, our father gave him the nickname Turtle Happy.

Rocks, bones, semi-precious stones, turtles, snakes—Flip loved and gathered them all. When we arrived at the museum, my brother solemnly presented the cache of precious things he had unearthed in fields near our home. The curator expressed lively interest and engaged my brother in conversation. My mother looked proud. I thought the adventure was rather wonderful too, compared to what happened regularly every day, which was far less exceptional. Even so, I didn't pay much attention to what they were talking about because I was daydreaming about the 94-foot long blue whale that was suspended from the museum's ceiling. I wanted to look more closely at that blue whale and I was doing my best to be patient while waiting for the moment when their conversation would end.

Finally, after what seemed a very long time, they finished their talking and we made our way to the whale exhibit. The blue whale was much more beautiful than the sperm whale in my picture book; it was unbelievably enormous. Spellbound, I lost track of my surroundings. I could hear that my mother and brother were continuing to talk about the visit with the curator, but their voices sounded far off, like sounds from another story entirely. Finally they got tired of standing around and wanted to leave. Of course

I didn't want to go. Looking at that blue whale gave me the same kind of feeling that I had when I sat at my window and looked out at the sky full of stars.

After that visit, I sometimes found myself daydreaming about the huge museum hall where the blue whale floated in mid air. In my daydreams the hall filled with water. Then the cords that held the whale dropped off, and the whale came alive. It quickened--swimming, leaping and turning through the dissolving roof of the museum into the metropolis itself. The great blue whale let loose on New York City!

The whole city filled with seawater, and it washed everything clean. It washed everything ugly away so that we could start over. Everyone was floating in the flood and they were happy, even more happy than we kids were when the brook behind our houses flooded and filled the streets with four feet of water and everyone got out their inner tubes and boats and sailed around, splashing and playing. Very happy, in other words. We want everything to be washed clean. We want everything ugly to be washed away. We want to start over.

Whales disappeared from my life and awareness for many years, surfacing again when I was in my late 20s. That summer, I was in Provincetown, an artists' community at the tip of Cape Cod. Cape Cod had once been a whaling center, but whales were not on my mind in any way. Instead I was in love with an Italian painter. I was researching a book on the underground press, and I was absorbed in the world of avant garde art.

One evening at a party I chatted with the host, an Armenian businessman who was married to a rather mediocre painter. Our conversation was unremarkable until the moment when out of nowhere he said firmly to me, "You shouldn't continue to be an editor and writer. You should be working with Nature, with living creatures like whales." I had no idea what had gotten into him. His pronouncement was completely unrelated to anything we had been discussing and in addition to that he wasn't the type of person who offered this kind of unsolicited, unusual advice. I remember how surprised I was and how I protested, insisting that I was quite happy with my life as an editor and writer, and had no interest in working with Nature or with whales. The incident would have faded into oblivion long ago, were it not for the fact that what the Armenian businessman Al Bodian urged me to do actually began to happen.

Yes, it turned out that he must have been very psychic, that at that particular moment he was channeling my future in a prophetic way because a few years later, I moved to California and settled in a small town called Bolinas, which means *whale* in Portuguese. And my adventure with whales picked up its pace.

My daughter Danielle and I made our first trip to Bolinas on the kind of day that makes you forget that there is any suffering in human life, a day defined by brisk air, big blue sky, and all the freshness and movement of early autumn. In our pale blue Plymouth Valiant with the word POETRY painted on the driver's side, we came over the softly rounded bosom of Mt. Tamalpais, winding down the hairpin turns of coastal Highway 1 until we reached the curved shoreline of Stinson Beach. We drove along the edge of the limpid blue water of Bolinas Lagoon, where white egrets nested in tall eucalyptus groves in a nearby canyon and flocks of pelicans circled and dove into the silky water. Past the lagoon, huge eucalyptus trees lined the road on either side as we approached the town.

Once I saw that place, I was done for. It was the fairytale town I had always longed for. Bolinas had a wonderful scent, a perfume mixed of the sea, pungent eucalyptus, wet earth, chaparral, seaweed, cows, horses, fish and roses. Its tiny downtown boasted a charming white clapboard church. There was an old-fashioned general store, a small cafe, a hardware store, a library, a seedily chic old hotel, a small post office, a bar that never seemed to empty, and a surfboard shop populated with a panoply of beautiful young guys. Bolinas was home to many poets and a mecca for artists, musicians, healers, cowboys, fishermen, craftspeople and unique wanderers. From the start, I felt very much at home there. It was a little town of 1200 people, called by some a hippie arcadia and by others a bohemian outpost. People knew each other very well. It was a strong community. You could run wild in Nature on the beaches and mesa, run wild creating art or just run wild with each other. And we did all of that. It was the early 70s, an intense, idyllic time, ornamented with its share of grief and excesses.

I arrived in Bolinas after a big oil spill in January 1971 washed thousands of gallons of bunker oil up on Bolinas beaches, killing hundreds of seabirds. The oil spill galvanized the Bolinasians. People had a shocking direct experience about how fragile the ecosystem was. They realized that they couldn't hide out in their coastal hamlet and escape from what was happening to the planet. Hundreds of volunteers converged to help with the clean-up and bird rescue. By the time the oil spill was cleaned up, Bolinas had hatched a new perspective about how to relate to community, environment and growth. It is one of a very few places that has actually managed to limit growth. The good news is that Bolinas remains adamant about preserving the natural environment, residents' independence and quality of life. But even so, the character of the town has changed because real estate prices have soared and only people of means can afford to buy anything. Not the way it used to be way back when I lived there, when life was so much more free-form and cheap.

Soon after I moved there, I met Joan McIntyre, an environmentalist who was in the process of starting Project Jonah,
which was the first organization dedicated to saving the
whales, years before the more long-lived and well-known
Greenpeace began. Project Jonah's coterie included some
of the counter-culture's heavy hitters. The seed money to
start the organization came from Stewart Brand, the creator
of the Whole Earth Catalog and later The Whole Earth
Review. Once we got rolling board member Jerry Mander,
who became well-known for his books *4 Arguments For the
Elimination of Television* and *In the Absence of the Sacred,* wrote
text for a full page ad that Project Jonah ran in the New York
Times. It was an expensive and very effective action that
magnetized tremendous attention and support to Jonah's
cause. Singers Judy Collins and David Crosby accepted
positions on the board of advisors. Poet Gary Snyder and
California Governor Jerry Brown were staunch supporters.
And there was Joan, orchestrating the whole music. She
already had one environmental coup to her credit, having
played a large part in the campaign that made it politi-
cally incorrect to wear furs. Now, she was well on her way
to making whales both a popular icon and a fashionable,
trendy cause.

I learned a great deal about how to create something from
nothing by watching Joan, who was imaginative, bold
and sometimes reckless. She dramatically embodied the

yearning, anger and disappointment that I had felt since I was a young girl when I dreamed of falling through the mirage of New Jersey into an untrammeled Indian paradise where I could live at one with Nature. Joan had her own version of that story. In the same skin with the articulate, powerful environmentalist that accomplished work for the whales each day, there lived a wild woman deeply disillusioned and disturbed by Western civilization.

After she left Project Jonah, she spent time with dolphins in Hawaii. She added an A to the end of her first name and became Joana. At the age of 58 she married a Fijiian fisherman 30 years her junior. I don't know how long she lived the life of a traditional Fijiian wife under the name Joana McIntyre Varawa. I can't imagine it lasting more than a few years. If she was anything like the person I knew when we worked together, that marriage must have been one wild trajectory for everyone involved, even if the Fijiians are as gentle and friendly as some people say. She wrote about the experience in a beautiful book titled *Changes in Lattitude: An Uncommon Anthropology,* but I know there was more to the story, unwritten things one could intuit between the lines.

In the Seventies whales became a symbol of the sacredness inherent in Nature. Scientists and poets alike spoke of them as emblems of deep knowing, record-keepers of some kind of ancient wisdom. This struck a chord in me, bringing me back to the picture of the sperm whale swimming in the night sea from my childhood storybook. When Joan McIntyre told me that she was looking for an assistant, of course I joined her crew. There are no coincidences, as some people are always pointing out.

Recently I ordered a copy of *Mind in the Waters*, an anthology of poems, essays and cetacean research that Joan assembled while she headed Project Jonah. I had always admired Joan's writing and I wanted to re-read some of the pieces she contributed to the book. Her essays were passionate and poetic. I found the poetry and stories contributed by others just as moving as I had years ago. Farley Mowat's account of a whale trapped in a cove and John Lilly's and William Curtsinger's essays about their experience with whales and dolphins were especially satisfying.

What are you looking for when you go back over these books from your Bolinas days? I asked myself not long ago. There is a fair amount of nostalgia to it, I have to admit. Not that I am a person averse to nostalgia, that mixture of happy sadness and longing for things past and gone. If I were, I never would have started this writing. After all, nostalgia has its uses. As Janelle L. Wilson suggests in her book *Nostalgia: A Sanctuary of Meaning,* the process of reminiscence involves a search for meaning, and nostalgia plays a part in it. Wilson writes, "…the acts of remembering, recalling, reminiscing and the corollary emotional experience of nostalgia may facilitate the kind of coherence, consistency and sense of identity that each of us so desperately needs…What meaning is being constructed in the retelling? What purpose is being served?"

Exactly. Or not quite exactly because I do wonder about Wilson's phrase "sense of identity that each of us so desperately needs." I don't feel particularly desperate for a sense of identity myself. That was something that tormented me decades ago but no longer perplexes me. I have arrived at a rough estimate of my identity. (I do not really exist anyway.) Here I am, take it or leave it. Actually, the leavetaking is somewhere on the horizon and it is approaching more closely all the time. The time for desperately seeking a sense of identity is in the past. Now it's time for letting go.

What is the buried meaning, what insights can be gained? This question is at the heart of recalling and of life review. Now that they are readily available on my bookshelf, I continue to peruse Orville Schell's book *The Town that Fought to Save Itself* and Joan's *Mind in the Waters*. I like looking through the photographs of friends, neighbors and lovers from 40 years ago, and recalling the zip and dip of our adventures together. My younger daughter is nearly as old as I was then. It's odd how quickly time passes; it's odd, interesting and surreal to grow old.

The whales themselves drew me to work with Joan. Both of us believed in their intelligence and the power of their mythic presence. Both she and I wanted to return to a more magical way of being where supernatural and ordinary realities could live easily with each other, where the whole of Nature could be experienced as sentient and intelligent. Each of us had had enough experience in those areas to know that this expanded reality is more authentic than the mechanistic view espoused by the overculture. "Animals were once, for all of us, teachers," Joan wrote in one essay. "They instructed us in ways of being and perceiving that extended our imaginations, that were models for additional possibilities."

I wonder where Joan is now. I hope she is happy, even though it never seemed a white environmentalist like her could really be too happy, because she knew so much about the erosion of Nature and the planet. Yet I remind myself that I have learned how to open to happiness, despite how much worse planetary and political conditions are today than they were 40 years ago. Hopefully she has learned to cultivate happiness, too.

To my mind, one brilliant, unique, somewhat difficult person is quite enough for any human being to deal with. But at that time, I was closely related to two of that species. Joan was one, and other was radical activist Keith Lampe, who had changed his name to Ponderosa Pine. Pine was a Korean War vet who became a peace activist and then moved on to take part in the Yippies, along with Abbie Hoffman, Paul Krasner and others. And now you're asking me who were the Yippies? Dear child, the Yippies were a bunch of revolutionary guys who wanted to change society. That's why they decided to take on the government, big business, the military, and whatever other powers that be. You can read about it in Abbie Hoffman's book *Revolution for the Hell of It.* When we met, Pine was post-Yippie. He had turned his attention to saving the Earth. A tall, thin, highly opinionated, caustic, long-haired, long-bearded guy, Pine went barefoot all year round as a political/spiritual statement. He didn't have a home, but made himself comfortable enough in the homes of a variety of people, some of whom found him fascinating and others, old friends, who gave him free rein in their houses.

My daughter Danielle couldn't stand him. "Why are you still hanging out with that weirdo, Mom?" she would question me vehemently, rolling her eyes to indicate how intolerable it was. Pine was not exactly what most 10-year girls have in mind as a household fixture, much less Mom's lover. He did little to discourage Danielle's contempt. Generally, he forded her disapproval by ignoring it, which infuriated her even more. And if you looked from where she and I stood talking with each other, you could see Pine walking barefoot down the road away from our house, loudly twanging Issa, the strange, 6- foot long one-stringed instrument that he named after his daughter, who was in turn named for the great Japanese haiku master.

Pine was walking along making his characteristic word-less sounds, which in my memory were usually not melodious, and often went something like HEEeeeyaaa hhheeeeee-e-e-e-aaaaahh. His head was bobbing up and down in self-affirmation and he had, as he often did, a bemused pothead smile on his face. By anyone's estima-tion, a real character.

Pine's keen intellect and his devotion to ideas, causes and strategies for social and environmental change were a big part of what attracted me to him. But he was not an easy person to deal with. One day he told me about a visit he recently had with his mother. She told him, "Keith, I hope that you find an opportunity that you can accept someday." He laughed when he recounted the incident, proud to be that recalcitrant. There were days when I felt as if Joan McIntyre and Ponderosa Pine were playing ping pong using me as a ball, because of course, those two brilliant beings saw things quite differently and did not approve of each other's methods, opinions and lifestyle. Joan thought I should break up with Pine whose presence was, in her opinion, a nuisance and an embarrassment to the environmental movement. Pine wanted me to stop working with Joan. He thought her a mercenary, ambitious environmental sell-out. I managed to navigate my own course between them most of the time, but it was not comfortable. Pine was a judgmental character, and when I fell out of grace with him, he would hiss at me. "You're nothing but a twerpy hustler!" Maybe I was, because I enjoyed tootling around with him on his grand schemes and projects. Or maybe he was simply describing his own shadow side. It's rather refreshing to look back at the movie from my current vantage point.

Our goal at Project Jonah was a world-wide whale-hunting moratorium. Joan traveled widely, speaking at environmental conferences, creating demonstrations and media attention that drew popular attention to the cause of the whales. My own work was not as glamorous or public, though it was far more enjoyable than some of the jobs I've had, which of course is another subject entirely and one that could be quite instructive and entertaining given the space. During much of the time I spent with Project Jonah, I worked in an office that had been added onto Joan's Bolinas home, with the sweep of the mesa before me as I looked out its windows. Taking a break from work often meant having lunch on the sunny deck, or walking down the back roads of Bolinas, past a fascinating display of quaint ramshackle houses and wonderful gardens interspersed with fields of tall grass. So it was what people call a good work environment.

For a year I developed and coordinated an international childrens' campaign to save the whales partnering with environmental organizations in seven countries. The poems, stories and drawings we collected from children all over the world pleaded with the Japanese to stop whaling. Boxes of them piled up in the office as the months went on. It was good work, ideologically, but it was basically administrative work. That's why it was so wonderful when at the end of the year Project Jonah's board surprised me by asking me to spend a month working in Japan as the first American to speak for the whales.

Except for the birth of my daughter Danielle, birthing being an activity of positively mythic proportions, life had provided me no other opportunity of such grand dimensions until then. Though that may be an overstatement, since being born in itself is such a mythic task. Now I was being asked to go to a foreign country and to galvanize popular attention and public opinion as broadly as I could. I had a mission but no obvious credentials other than my status as a Project Jonah staff member and a collection of environmental articles I had penned for various magazines. Not that I was intimidated. I knew I could do the job. I felt quite capable of communicating widely. I also knew that

I would have a lot of help, even though I had no idea of where it would come from. Of course, I was excited about going. Underneath the excitement, a wonderful layer of confidence and trust streamed through. It was clear that this mission was so much bigger than me. I had to surrender into the stream. I felt as if I had stepped over a threshold into another theater.

Two things happened before I left. One was a meeting and one was a dream and they were intertwined. In the dream, I was flying high above the ocean. The sun was on the water, throwing thousands of diamond lights into the air with each wave. My daughter Danielle and I had taken on the bodies of birds but kept our own human heads, something that seems amusing as I write it, but which was perfectly natural at the time. We flew effortlessly, swerving and turning in space, surrounded by an endlessly unfolding display of clouds. Looking down, I saw that far below us, seven huge sperm whales were surfacing one at a time. They spouted, one after the other, as if each had a particular note to sound. The sun was shining on their huge bodies. Their quiet exaltation was beautiful. Yet something was missing. I turned to my daughter and said, "But there must be eight to play music for the Precious Jewel." She just looked back at me, saying nothing. Then, the eighth whale surfaced. Eight whales, I thought to myself, what an auspicious offering.

Even now, nearly 40 years later, remembering that dream makes me feel happy. Everything about it was ecstatic, free of the trammels of ordinary reality. The immense expanse of the sea, the vast reaches of the sky, the way light streamed and cascaded from the ocean to the sky, all opened up my mind and heart to simply being, free of thought. What ecstatic release, floating weightless on currents of wind, completely relaxed in a boundless expanse, with the sensation of wind and sun on my feathered, winged body.

And the way those gigantic sperm whales surfaced slowly, one after the next, like a processional coming up from the depths to make a sacred offering of their appearance. When they spouted, their water offerings were celebratory, like yogis throwing rice up into the air at the end of a meditation practice. When I woke up in the morning, I was invigorated by that dream, which seemed like a blessing on the journey I was about to make. I thought to myself that morning, *"I am really fortunate. I have just met an amazing Tibetan master, and I am on my way to Japan to work for the benefit of the whales."*

I had just met an amazing Tibetan master. He was a Rinpoche, or *Precious Jewel*, a title given to Tibetan tulkus. *Tulkus* are teachers that through the force of their spiritual development have the power to choose the time and place of their next lifetime; they consciously reincarnate in order to continue their spiritual work. Sometimes they leave letters at the time of their death foretelling the place where they will be reborn and giving the names of their future parents. If they leave no letter or message, their disciples begin to search. When a small child is found who has some of the signs of a *tulku*, the child is tested. Several ritual bells and several rosaries may be shown, among them the rosary and bell of the previous incarnation.

If the child chooses the objects that belonged to the previous incarnation, the search may be over. Later, I read and heard many stories about how tulkus are found. But that day, as I prepared to join my friends at the door of the Rinpoche's residence, I knew nothing about it. I had never met a real spiritual teacher. *(As you may already have noticed, even though our country was founded on freedom of religion, we really have no tradition of wandering yogis or consciously reborn masters.)* I was nervous. I worried about being seen through, all my faults and limitations lit up by the lamp of the lama's insight. As I discovered in the months that followed, that was a justified concern.

Seven of us went to play music for the lama that day. Ponderosa Pine, the organizer of the visit, hoped that there would be eight of us to represent the noble eight-fold path of Buddhism, but as so often happens in human endeavors, we fell short by one. I remember how the lama sat on a seat by the window with the sun outlining his form, making his golden skin even more golden. He wore a long brocade robe with a beautiful silk shirt underneath. I thought that the colors of his clothing and the fabric of which they were made were daringly beautiful, the kind of clothing one would certainly find in another, more refined world.

I remember the sound of our music, a fairly haphazard improvisation, not unpleasant, something like a conversation among friends. It went along well enough most of the time. The lama even played with us for awhile. But there were moments when the sound blurred and throbbed as if it was unwinding into waves, and I couldn't hear any music in it at all. I felt as if I was hearing the minds of the musicians or what was speaking from their psyches through the music. At those moments, I experienced a pang of despair because we seemed like a group of lost souls on a raft in the middle of the ocean. So it went back and forth, the not unpleasant musical conversation suddenly unraveling into strange waves of sound, and on those waves floated our small boat of lost souls far from any shore.

That was unsettling enough, but it was not the only unusual thing that happened. The solidity of physical appearances trembled; the colors and shapes within the room throbbed and pulsed as if they were under a strobe light. It was disorienting and disturbing. The thing that bothered me most was the way people's faces became so variable. Their faces became unfixed; other faces passed through them. It went back and forth. The music unraveled into energy, physical appearances pulsated and disintegrated, then sound and appearances gathered again as if nothing had occurred to disturb what we consider to be ordinary reality.

When you take LSD, you anticipate the possibility that strange phantasmagoria may arise. You expect things to be all bent out of shape, pulsating like a pointillist painting, blossoming one thing from the next in an impossible profusion of images and thoughts. But that day with the Rinpoche, there was no hallucinogenic substance. It seemed to take a great deal of concentration to keep breathing and to playing the music as my habitual view of reality shifted, broke apart and reformed. I don't know what I would have done if the lama had not been there. As I struggled to deal with my profound discomfort, I found his presence steadying. Actually, I doubt that any of it would have happened without the lama. When I thought about it afterwards, it seemed that in some way his presence allowed it to happen. Would visible reality have unraveled in the way it had without the lama's presence? Did he catalyze that experience somehow, purposely or just by his state of being? Questions, many questions arose in my mind after our visit.

What was the function of a lama anyway? I wondered what it meant to have a spiritual teacher and if I had one, what I would have to give up in the process. The subject of giving up anything at all made me anxious (though of course there were a great many things I wished I could jolly well get rid of). The thought of giving up my autonomy and independence terrified me. I was afraid that was what one might have to do in order to obey a spiritual teacher.

Coincidentally, I had just finished reading the life story of the famous Tibetan yogi Milarepa, whose spiritual accomplishments came only after great exertion, struggle and despair. Milarepa's teacher Marpa commanded that Milarepa build many complex structures. No sooner would Milarepa finish one than Marpa would order him to destroy it. Oh, how impossible I thought, reading about it. How could I ever stand up to those kinds of rigors? Milarepa must have had a lot of faith. He must have understood what he was looking for. He must have believed that Marpa could help him find it. Whereas I did not have faith, not in any religion or any teacher. I did not know what I was looking for.

Once I thought I knew what I was looking for, in the days when I knelt in church praying for the beautiful statues to come alive and speak to me. I wanted to have a talk, possibly more than one talk, with Jesus, or perhaps the Virgin Mary. I was certain that I needed some directions. It seemed best to go right to the source. I prayed and prayed, but statues never spoke and Jesus or Mary never appeared in a blaze of radiance. I lost faith. I gave up. I grew up. I espoused my own religions-- atheism, nihilism, hedonism. I may have become a woman with no faith, but I still had a profound longing for mystical experience and divine communion. Underneath the protective veneer, I was searching for the deeper meaning of my life. That's why the visit to the Rinpoche unsettled me on many levels.

His spiritual magnetism was evident. But how did I know he was real or trustworthy? How did I know that Buddhism had anything to do with me? Then there was the matter of the strange stuff that happened when we went to play music there. I wondered whether the pulsating reality was not just a hallucinogenic fluke, something that happened because you took a drug, but more like the way things really are. I found the thought both fascinating and deeply subversive. Because if reality was not solid, what was there to rely upon? Why should I rely upon reality so completely, if it was just a mirage? And then, of course the next question naturally arose. Was I a mirage, too? So that is how the stage was set as I prepared to go to Japan for a month to work on behalf of the whales.

When I arrived in Tokyo, the day was cold and gray. The air was incredibly polluted; it muffled the landscape of the city, draining its color. Groups of young children walked to school, book bags in hand. They wore surgical masks as a protective gesture against the foul air. With their heads bowed and their little masks, they looked like the shades in Dante's Purgatorio making their way through the miasmic veils of a dim land. It was horrible to see them reduced to such a plight. I thought of my own daughter, who was breathing the clean salty air of Bolinas. If she were going to school, she would be walking down the road under big eucalyptus trees to the pretty white schoolhouse. In Tokyo, I was afraid to breathe a deep breath.

I was received as a distinguished visitor and introduced to some of the country's leading writers, artists and political activists. One of my jobs was to get media coverage. I did my best. I was featured on the cover of the Japanese version of Business Week and secured feature articles in all the other major Japanese newspapers, as well as landing an Associated Press piece that made its way into newspapers in many countries, gaining considerable visibility for the cause of the whales.

Although I was busy day and night talking about the whales, my month in Tokyo had a stark solitary quality. Each evening when I returned to my tiny apartment, I'd sit at the dining table, think about the day's events and look at the pink bookmark-shaped paper that the Rinpoche had given me. I had put it up on a mirror near the table. At times I spoke the words on that pink paper out loud. *Om Ah Hung Vajra Guru Padma Siddhi Hung.* They were printed in blue ink. I did not understand them, but they comforted me. There were days when the sun in the polluted Tokyo sky was as red as blood. I sat at the window and cried at the suffering of the world.

One day, two American models befriended me. They were tall, slender, blond, and very much in love with each other. My borrowed apartment was in a drab modern building, but they lived in a wonderful series of ancient rooms that had antique wall coverings and ornamental woodwork. One of their rooms opened out onto a small garden. Its pond was filled with golden fish, but its surface was almost completely covered with fallen leaves. Stands of bamboo bordered the garden. On one side stood many statues of the Buddha; most of them were headless. The garden, they told me, had been part of a temple. But now the temple was closed and the priest had taken another job. When they went inside to cook dinner, I cleaned the leaves off the surface of the pond. Watching the gold fish swim, I thought about the headless Buddhas and sighed.

Finally my month in Tokyo was over. I was tired, and I had to concede that there was something very ironic about a woman wanting to save the whales who had never seen a

whale in her life. I wanted to see a whale, more than anything. I decided to stop in Hawaii to rest, knowing that
humpback whales frequented the waters around those
islands. It was strange, plunging from the cold Tokyo winter
that was just on the verge of spring into the hot Hawaiian
sun with only the stale air of the airplane in between. The
brown, round Hawaiians playing ball on the beach had a
wonderful grace and openness. I could see them drinking
beer at the sides of their small wood frame houses, which
were like an afterthought between motels.

I was ashamed to be white. I grew restless and agitated.
I wished I could find a doorway back into a slower, more
holy way of life. I looked at the tourists with their shopping
bags and snorkels, buying souvenirs to remember the time
they skimmed the surface of paradise and I looked at the
Hawaiians, and I became sick at heart.

More than anything, I wanted to see a whale. That was
the medicine I needed. I went out to the beach and lay
on the white sand. I listened to the rustle of the iron-
wood trees and watched the bright blue water stretching
out in the sun. I wasn't much on praying then. The idea
made me really uncomfortable. But it seemed more real-
istic than anything else I could think of then so I decided
to pray for the whales to come. Feeling small and timid,
I sat under the feathery trees and prayed. "Great whales,

I have worked for your protection, so that your tribes may increase. I come here in peace wishing for a sight of you. In my whole life, I have never seen you. Please come to me now."

The heat rose in waves from the sand. Time passed in a welcome monotony. I scanned the brilliant ocean for a sign. Things slowed and fell away. Finally, far off, the back of a whale glistened for an instant in the sun. Can you imagine how I felt? I jumped up. Then I sank back down on the sand again. "This is just you and me talking, whale. I am simple. Simple."

Three whales curved up and slipped back into the water again. All I saw was a glimpse of their backs. It was like glimpsing something you've loved for a long time, at last. I peered into the ocean as if it were my own eyes. "What whales are you?" I asked. "Show me. I want to keep you close to me." Time slowed. Then an incredibly beautiful huge humpback whale rose vertically up out of the water, held, and slid back down again. I felt myself click into a focus of unusual clarity. I was very calm. When the whale rose again, my eye was a fine lens. Time it seemed had stopped entirely. The whale was far out on the ocean, but to me it appeared to be very close, three or four feet away. I saw it clearly. Each detail of its form appeared with precise definition. Its eye looked into my own from an ancient wordless place.

When you have an epiphany, it does not last forever. You may still be shining from inside out, but you find yourself getting up from that place on the beach. You prayed for whales and they answered. You are changed, and you still have to get up and walk down the beach back to your motel. Sooner or later, you pack your bag and prepare to return home. The experience may resonate within for a long time, perhaps even for the rest of your life, but the work of everyday living calls you back, and you have to go into mundane practice, where the fields are prepared for planting and the alchemical substances are distilled, where the swiss chard is steamed and the floor swept.

I melted back into the yin embrace of Bolinas and to my life there. Danielle and I moved from our house on the mesa into a tiny cabin. It was just a wooden shack set under plum trees next to a creek—small and primitive, but homey enough. Life was so easy then, not just because I was young. You could live on very little, and that left plenty of time just to be. It was relaxing to live simply and still have enough. We had more than enough in many ways. Danielle had a pony. The small country school in Bolinas suited her well. I found work as a cashier in the town's general store, a fine job that allowed me to meet and greet the locals and pay the bills, too.

That's when I changed my name to Blackbird. Like most people, I was given a name when I was born. It was Gail Melissa Emaus. I was given those names, and when you are given names, you're expected live with them, which I did, except for taking the name Madonia when I married Michael M. But I was tired of my names, both given and married. I wanted to choose a name that I could tap into and learn from, one that would propel me into a deep association with another form of life. One day as I sat looking the needles on the pine trees shaking and shining in the sun, a blackbird appeared and perched in one tree, its feathers like rainbows in the sunlight.

Blackbirds are not endangered. Nobody is trying to save them. They are not viewed as noble or special like the eagle, raven or whale. They are everywhere, like factory workers, ditch diggers, waiters, waitresses, subway riders. I decided to change my name to Blackbird. One thing I learned pretty soon. You better be ready for whatever is hidden inside your name.

Four months after I took the name Blackbird, thousands and thousands of blackbirds descended on Richard Nixon's Maryland home. (He was President then.) It really took me back a bit. I mean, I never liked Nixon much, but I had no idea it was so obvious. I lay in bed at night pondering that oracular plague of wings on his roof. Of course, there was a logical reason for it. Blackbirds had multiplied. They could survive when other species could not. But even the blackbirds were feeling there wasn't much of a place to live in anymore. And that is why they descended en masse, prophetic messengers that they are, to talk to Nixon. Of course, Nixon wasn't much on interspecies communication. He didn't even communicate well within his own species. So he didn't understand what the blackbirds were trying to say to him. The Army was called in, and they attempted to kill the birds by spraying them with a detergent called Tergitol. But the birds flew away before they could do it.

"Let your life be a friction against the machine," Thoreau wrote. Those millions of blackbirds were such a friction. A few months later, 14 million blackbirds descended on Army bases in Kentucky and Tennessee. The Army assured the public that the Tergitol would not harm humans or the environment. It would simply strip the oil from the blackbirds' feathers, so they would all freeze to death. They succeeded in killing 2 million. Two million blackbirds. I felt like an interspecies crossbreed, suspended between two worlds.

I wish I still had a copy of the tiny newspaper article published soon after that massacre. It wasn't even about the

Army and the blackbirds. Instead, it reported that some very *Biiig* blackbirds had been seen, in some other part of the country. So many years later, I wonder, did I make that up? I don't believe I did, but in retrospect it seems to belong in one of those tabloids that specialize in odd news. Very Big Blackbirds. It made me nervous. I thought that maybe the Big Blackbirds were the spirit protectors of all those birds that the Army killed. I thought maybe they would come and take me away to the Big Blackbird Spirit Place and they would call me to task.

"Why did you just sit there?" they would ask me. "Why didn't you do anything to save your brothers and sisters?" And there would be nothing I could say. Why did I choose that name? I couldn't figure it out. I asked my friend Ponderosa Pine the question one day. Just then, in that strange pixillating way the Universe has, a blackbird flew in through the open door of the house. It flew around and around the room, its beating wings stirring the air. Then it found the door and disappeared. Its beating wings and yellow eyes were answer enough to my question.

These events--the coincidental appearance of the blackbird, the meeting with the Tibetan master, the dream of the eight whales, and the way the whales appeared in answer to my prayer in Hawaii all seemed like talismans of another kind of reality. I turned them over and over, as if in thinking about them, I could figure them out. I had yearned for a more magical, expansive reality for years but when those emblems arose like harbingers, I was both thrilled and afraid. There is a great comfort in the familiar conventional world. I had no idea where my search for something more would take me.

That year, I believe it was 1974, was filled with unusual experiences. I haven't had a year quite like it since then. One summer afternoon Magda Cregg came to visit me at my cabin by the creek and we smoked some potent hash. Magda was like a force of nature--colorful, fierce, and indomitable. We called her "the woman's guru" because she presided over our peyote circles and orchestrated many aspects of feminine culture. Magda lived with poet Lew Welch before he mysteriously disappeared, never to be seen again, and later she became known as the mother of rock star Huey Lewis, but Huey was barely a teenager then.

Magda was a provocative woman. She liked to rock the boat. In fact, she was devoted to it. She was also an aficionado of aphrodisiacs from various lands, disappearing regularly on expeditions for actual field research, then bringing back stories of her adventures to us at home. Magda was in her 40s, and I was about a decade younger. I remember vividly one moment on the beach with her.

As we lay naked next to each other, she bitterly complained about the unfairness of gender prejudice. Now that she was aging, she told me angrily, it was difficult to find men willing to be her sexual partner, while as men aged, they continued to attract young women. What she said didn't make any sense to me then, but now, I understand much better.

The day that Magda came to visit, poetry was stuck in my craw. The trouble was simple. I wanted poets to assume immense mythic presence like Orpheus, singing great songs that brought even trees to speak. Instead, I had to watch Bolinas poets with cool eyes and self-satisfied smiles read lines that reminded me how very white and dry we were. Speaking of white, maybe I should blame it on Robert Graves. I was reading his book *The White Goddess* then. What stuck with me was this passage. *"European poetic lore is indeed ultimately based on magical principles, the rudiments of which formed a close religious secret for centuries but which were at last garbled, discredited and forgotten. Now it is only by accident that poets make their lines magically potent in the ancient sense."*

There it was! That was my problem in a nutshell. Once poets embodied a mystic lineage of sacred Sound and Word. Poetry was a living river from which all people drank. It was not removed and dried out. It did not shuffle like a wary captive. It was not starved, abandoned or scoffed at. No! It was a fountain of the divine, an illuminating fire. How I wanted language of such divine fire to manifest powerfully in the midst of modern life, and in me!

That's what was stuck in my craw the day Magda came to visit. I believed I had an ally in Magda because she, it seemed, also wanted poets to break out of their bloodless confines. As we sat smoking the hash in a clearing near the creek, I complained about the poets who lived all around--how they got obnoxiously drunk and made fools of themselves in the bar, how they held themselves aloof like ice queens, how they panted after influence. I couldn't stand their shopping list, teacup poetry, all decay and refinement. They were so effete.

I poured my frustration out into her ears and Magda grew impatient. Seeing her face change, I found myself wishing that I had not begun to speak at all. But it was too late. She was already leaning forward with one elbow on her leg and her arm extended, in a pose reminiscent of Picasso's portrait of Gertrude Stein. It seemed to me that Magda hissed when she spoke. And what she hissed was "You must *sing* your songs!"

I was stunned. Sing my songs? What did this mean? I sat there, tangling my fingers around each other and laughing nervously. The rest of our visit bleared by. I don't remember what else we talked about, if indeed we talked of anything.

When she left and I was alone in the dirt of the clearing, I went back to what she had said. Sing my songs. There was an ache in me, like something that had been held in for too long. If that ache was my unsung songs, it seemed terrifying to let them out. But I wondered what I really had to lose.

The purple leaves of the plum trees, the sound of the water in the creek, the sun on the water, the heat all pulsed in dancing patterns of light. I lost my sense of time. Then something happened that surprised me. A blazing column of white light descended into the top of my head and filled my whole being, saturating me with its intense radiance. As I was filled, something released in my voice. I didn't even know I had anything like it in me. And I wasn't sure whether it was me at all, in the way we think of qualities being ours so particularly and possessively. It was beyond language, wordless, calling out as primal sound in a voice I had never heard before--unearthly, like Celtic keening, like the cantillation of ancient priests and priestesses, something mysterious and holy.

I thought to myself in a mixture of shock and joy, *It's the mythic presence!* For three hours, I sang, laughed, cried and even rolled in the dirt. I just didn't care who thought what about it. No one was there to hear or see it anyway, except the birds, the trees, the grass and the water. The sheer power of that voice was amazing. It was truly beautiful, though not in the ordinary sense. It was as if an ancient being lived within me who had awakened to sing her songs again. And once she started to sing them, she forgot herself entirely and simply became the music.

We speak of *finding one's voice* as a way of describing the self-understanding and strength that comes from embodying oneself in an authentic way. I had certainly been trying to find my voice in just that way for years. But the voice that made itself heard after Magda left me that day was bigger and deeper than any of my ideas about my self. The vibration of that voice opened me up and aired me out like a great gust of wind from the old days. It was a pathway to other times and different states of mind. Ah, I thought in between long rich breath lines, where has this been all my life? That year, the Universe showered me with gifts. Certainly that wonderful voice was a gift but it was a gift I did not receive easily.

That voice was too potent for comfort, too powerful, undiluted, provocative -- as strange as something from another realm. It had depth, grandeur, richness and breadth. There was longing in it too, a grieving that was terrible to hear, like a yearning soul crying out its prayer to merge with the divine, or singing what it knows of the sorrows all beings share. The naked creative power in the voice that came to me had nothing to do with striving, armor or being limited to one's current personality. I was afraid of its openness, limitlessness, interconnectedness.

How ironic it is. That's what I think when I remember this time. Wanting to expand out into more spacious experience, then shrinking up in fear at the enormous power of it. How safe it seems to stay with what is familiar, rather than taking the leap into the unknown. I wanted the big mythic knowledge, and I wanted to hang onto my little self. That was my struggle. I grappled with it as I lived my ordinary hours and days, sweeping the clearing in front of the cabin, making dinner, walking out on the mesa with the wind making waves in the tall grass, looking at the stars, having affairs, studying healing, swimming, writing poetry, working at the general store in Bolinas, that sweet refuge of a village, one of the most beautiful places I've had the pleasure to inhabit.

Nor can I report that I have finished the work of letting go of the little self. I wish I could say that. Then again, if I were done, would I be bragging about it? No, I would be way past bragging about my accomplishments, spiritual or otherwise. I think that when that time comes, it will be a blessed relief. Or maybe by then the idea of blessed relief will be in the past, too.

Even though the notion of finding a spiritual teacher filled me with what sometimes seemed equal parts of elation and dread, I started to study with Tarthang Tulku Rinpoche. The first seminar I signed up for was Dream Yoga. Believing that the seminar would take place at the lama's residence, where we had gone to play music, I arrived promptly at its grand door, excited about beginning my studies. But the person that answered the door told me that the seminar was not at Pema Ling, but at the Nyingma Institute, across town.

I walked quickly toward the Institute. My body felt light and insubstantial. Each step seemed the unreal step of an unreal person on unreal ground. The streets and the people on the streets, which were after all the people and streets of my everyday life, lost their vivid living quality, and seemed distant, like mere reflections. Remembering the musical gathering at which I first met Tarthang Tulku, I wondered if this sense of unreality was something that he specialized in. Yet what could he possibly have to do with my walk from the residence to the Institute?

Though each step seemed as if it was going nowhere, I finally arrived at the Nyingma Institute, an impressive rectangular building set high on a hill with a wonderful view of the city. I stood in the entryway for a moment, out of breath from my exertions. Surprisingly, I was not late. Inside, the atmosphere was quite peaceful. I registered and walked into the large room where the seminar was to be held, a room that was quite majestic, with tall ceilings and large windows. Hung high on its walls were black and white photographs of Tibetan spiritual masters. Each face conveyed so much depth, imparting to that otherwise ordinary room a palpable sense of history and lineage, much as portraits of ancestors give to an old family's manse. But this was no ordinary ancestral lineage, the masters in those photographs seemed to say as they looked down upon the room filled with well-dressed, talkative people.

The seminar participants occupied themselves in a convivial way as they waited to the lama to arrive. Neophyte that I was, I had no idea that Tarthang Tulku's seminars and books were attracting the attention of well-known scientists, psychologists, artists and doctors. That first seminar, and other later gatherings I participated in, were quite stimulating.

When the lama arrived in the room, he was as resplendent as he had been the first time I saw him. A handsome man with golden skin, close-cropped black hair, and a magnetic Venusian quality, he was eloquent, poetic, incisive and more spontaneous than anyone I had ever met. In his presence, all the windows of your psyche were flooded with light. Whether you liked it or not, because he didn't turn it on and off. He was that way all the time.

As the seminar began, he spoke of the illusory nature of outer appearances. The world is as much a dream as the dreams we create during sleep, he told us. Dream yoga was a method that we could train in to recognize that we were in a dream while in the midst of night time dreaming. Then, he said, we could change the context and the characters in the dream, or dissolve the dream entirely. I found this idea tremendously exciting.

After the talk was finished, we were led downstairs into a large room whose walls were painted bright green with red trim, a color scheme outrageous by conventional Western standards, but one that I found comforting. The room's unusual colors and the thangka paintings of spiritual masters on its walls gave permission to suspend our usual expectations.

Then Tarthang Tulku spoke about mantra, the sacred formulas used to address and invoke the energies and presence of enlightened ones. We learned about Padmasambhava, the Indian mystic who brought Buddhism from India to Tibet in the 5th century CE. When the lama led us in chanting, I realized with a start that the words of the mantra that we were chanting were the same words as those on the paper that he had given me before I went to Japan. *Om Ah Hung Vajra Guru Padma Siddhi Hung.* That in itself was dreamlike.

Some of the things I remember best from my studies with Tarthang Tulku were not recorded in any of the notes I took. During one seminar, when 30 or so participants were seated on meditation cushions in the downstairs room, Tarthang Tulku asked everyone simply to chant the syllable AH for 5 minutes, one breath after the next, with no melody. It should have been straightforward enough, but after a couple of minutes went by, I began to feel as if I was in a lunatic asylum. It was excruciating, a kind of bedlam, to hear in each of our voices the cacophony of our desires and thoughts. Did everyone hear our awful music as I did, and were they not letting on, but just chanting their AHs and pretending everything was perfectly balanced and harmonious, rather than the raw, pitiful vocal expose of what lay beneath our cool, calm exteriors? I wondered.

Was this experience—so similar to the one that happened when we went to play music for the lama-- happening because I was for another brief moment hearing myself and others as the lama heard us? I concluded that it must be so. I couldn't figure out any other way to explain it. How could the lama hear all that suffering so clearly and yet remain so calm and open? I wanted to be open in that way, to unlearn everything I had learned. I wanted to surrender my habit of recoiling in horror from my own pain, my habit of trying to protect myself from the suffering of others.

In another seminar, as the whole group was lying down on mats doing a visualization practice, I was surprised to see a fierce black image begin to form over the solar plexus of the petite, dark-haired woman who lay to the left of me. The image, surrounded with a shimmering halo of light, was dancing with arms raised up. In that moment, I had no idea whether I was seeing right. Was the image was really there?

The woman meanwhile, gazed down her body. She was looking at something, but was she seeing what I saw? She looked at me. "Do you see something?" she asked, nodding toward her abdomen. "Yes," I responded. Coincidentally, the lama passed by. The woman excitedly described the dancing figure, which was so beautiful, bright and fierce. She asked him what it was. What did it have to do with her? Why had it appeared? What did it mean? Was it real?

Overall, the lama seemed unimpressed. He suggested that the woman relax. It was not as if he denied what we saw -- he simply and deftly deflated our infatuation. She was very disappointed. She wanted there to be more. I wanted there to be more, too. It was such an intense, unfamiliar event. Perhaps our excitement was in the way. Maybe it just wasn't time for us to know anything more about it.

I found the teachings so inspiring that I wanted to devote myself to spiritual activities. In order to be closer to the lama and his efforts, I volunteered to work at Dharma Publishing, the company that was part of his work, where texts of great Tibetan masters were being translated and published. I enjoyed working there. I felt that I was doing something of real benefit. Things went along nicely for awhile, but one day my comfortable reality unraveled. We had been instructed to design our pages so that images of spiritual teachers remained intact, out of respect. The images were not to be divided or cut by a fold of the paper. But somehow, that is precisely what had happened. There was the famous teacher Nagarjuna, folded in half on our upcoming brochure.

I had not done the deed myself. The woman I worked with had created the layout. But as I came to learn again that day in a quite visceral way, one can be guilty by association, or one can simply be in the right place at the right time to become the recipient of some severe grace. When the whole drama began, I was sitting at my work place taking a little break by gazing at an image of the sacred syllable AH on the wall. One of my co-workers came in and told me that the lama wanted to see me. I could tell that something was wrong by the nervous tone of his voice. I entered the room where the lama was sitting with the offending brochure in his hand, surrounded by a sizable group of workers. Everyone looked at me in a concerned way, as if I was about to be executed. At least that was my interpretation of the situation. I approached and without thinking, knelt down in front of the lama. He was very stern. With a metal ruler, he pointed to the image of Nagarjuna.

"Look at this," he said. "Oh," I said, very surprised that I was being viewed as the guilty party when I knew I had nothing to do with it. Immediately I began to erect my defenses. "That's not right, I know. But I didn't do that," I sputtered. I should say before proceeding further that I trusted the lama. I was in awe of the lama and I was afraid of his power, but I trusted him. The lama took the metal ruler and moved it in a slow arc toward my head. I was convinced that I might die at that moment, that he might simply split my head open with that ruler, so powerful was his presence. And at that moment I thought, "Well, if I am not guilty of cutting Nagarjuna's image in half with the fold of the paper, I am certainly guilty of other actions. And if I do die now, this will be a very good way to die." Of course, my assessment of the situation turned out to be too easy to be true. I was not getting off the hook that simply. As I looked up, the lama had withdrawn the ruler and was looking at me coldly.

"Get out," he said loudly. "Get out right now!" I was astounded. How could he do this? I was not even guilty. The meek disciple disappeared and someone else took her place. That person was filled with tremendous rage at the unfairness of it all. "I will go!" I proclaimed loudly. I was on fire.

"Good," the lama said, as if pleased to be rid of me. Coursing with anger I went back to my work area, where only moments before I had been sitting blissfully gazing at the sacred syllable AH on the wall.

I packed up my things and walked out of there. Just before I got to the front door, I heard the lama's voice coming out of a dark room nearby. How could that possibly be? And what in the world was he saying? I couldn't make out the words. His voice was powerful, mesmerizing. It was eerie hearing it issue out of the dark room. Was I imagining it? Like so many of the events that occurred in my relationship with that lama, I wasn't sure. I was shocked at what was happening to me. I was filled with anger, despair and confusion.

I needed some time to think, to cool off. I decided to walk back to Berkeley. It turned out to be quite an amazing journey. It was as if someone had turned up the volume on my senses. The brick walls, the endless blue sky, the sounds of the train, the cars, houses, factories, people's faces, their little gardens, dogs, stones, everything pierced me with its beauty. In spite or perhaps because of the rage coursing through me, the beauty I experienced in the lama was in everything. I passed one tree that was as exquisite as a Chinese princess and stood in front of it, admiring its delicate foliage, its perfect shape, its scent, the way the breeze delicately riffled its leaves, and I felt ecstatic.

What is this? I asked myself. This spaciousness, this joy. Shouldn't I feel terrible, being sent away and then getting so angry about it? Instead I felt incredibly free and open. It was confusing. Later, the bliss faded and I found myself feeling unhappy and excluded. Determined to prove that I was worthy and that I was not a quitter, I spent the next six months trying to get back into the lama's good graces. Finally, in what seemed to be admittance by attrition, I managed to arrange a volunteer position for myself in public relations. The lama was not involved. I accomplished my effort through another student. Soon I had succeeded in interesting a prominent author in the lama and his work, and the author was going to write a book about Tibetan Buddhism, mentioning the lama, which he did. Later the book became quite successful. I was proud of myself.

One day I was sitting at a desk in the small sunny office where I worked at the Institute when the lama came into the room. I had not had direct contact with him since my last day at the publishing company. He looked at me and frowned. "What you doing here?" he asked accusingly. His question threw me into a tizzy and it was not only because of what was happening at that moment.

I had been asking myself that same question for so many years. What am I doing here? And underneath that, am I *allowed* to be here, to be alive? But finally, I heard myself responding woodenly, "I'm helping with the public relations," as if this literal explanation would resolve everything that boiled below the surface. "Oh," the lama said, suddenly uninterested. He turned and went out of the room.

There was so much energy coursing through my body that I thought I would pass out. My whole body shaking, I bent over slowly towards the ground as the fear began to drain out of me through my hands and feet. Breathing and letting go, the pent up energy poured out of me. It took a long time before I felt grounded again. Both of these experiences, though deeply uncomfortable at the time, seemed very purifying. I am grateful for them and for the other fierce, magical and profound teachings I received during that time.

There are many stories that accumulate around spiritual teachers. One of the stories that accumulated around Tarthang Tulku Rinpoche left a lasting impression on me. The story is about death. Two young women who lived near the lama's residence knocked on his door, distraught. They wanted to talk with the lama because their father had just died with a tormented expression on his face. His daughters found that expression unbearably painful. They came to ask if there was anything that they could do to help their father. The lama went upstairs. When he came back, he held in his hand a round mandala made of several kinds of metal. Tarthang Tulku gave them the round disc and told them to put it on their father's heart. He gave them a simple prayer to recite. They returned an hour later, very happy. As soon as they put the mandala on their dead father's chest, they reported, his body relaxed, and the expression on his face changed to a peaceful one.

What changed the torment of a dead man to peace? Was it the metal mandala? The lama's inner training? The daughters' faith? Or some mix of all of that? These were the questions I asked in the months after I heard the story. And though no one ever gave me an answer that could pass for scientific, I didn't care, for the event itself described the kind of science I valued.

The activities of the lama were fascinating to me. He wanted to tear up the parking lot behind the Nyingma Institute and create a garden. Before the garden work began, he decided to sponsor a celebration of the Buddha's birth in the parking lot. First a large, square three-tiered altar was built. Each side was at least 10 feet long. Its highest tier was over 6 feet tall. When everything was done, the altar, covered with beautiful cloth, flowers, fruit offerings, and countless candles, was resplendent. The crescent moon was high in the sky and a big crowd of disciples, lamas, and other invited guests had gathered. Various people, including eminent scholars such as the famous Tibetan translator Herbert Guenther, spoke.

I have forgotten their words, but I still recall what a beautiful light the myriad candles made, and how splendid the altar offerings appeared. Near the end of the event, Tarthang Tulku gave a talk. It was a thoroughly engaging speech, yet I remember only the last part of the last sentence. I imagine that the first part of the sentence went something like what Longchenpa said long ago, "Since everything is an apparition, having nothing to do with good or bad, acceptance or rejection, one might well burst out in laughter…" I know it was something like that. At the end of the sentence Tarthang Tulku said, "so now everyone give a big laugh!" And everyone did.

When they laughed, everything disappeared from my field of vision. The assembled guests, the altar, the moon, building, trees—all of it vanished. What took their place were brilliant planes of emerald green light. Shining richly, in a sparkling flow, plane after plane of blazing green radiance pervaded every corner of my imagination and sight, eclipsing with its brightness the forms of the ordinary world. As the emerald green light suffused my cells and pores, I forgot those who was near me, and stood there like a blind person having an inexplicable ecstatic vision. Could I have spoken then? It seemed that the distance between the experience and saying anything about it was very long, too long for any words to reach the surface and emerge. How long the green light lasted, I have no way of knowing. Some events take place in another kind of time altogether. Perhaps all events take place in another kind of time, perhaps there is no time, and some events free us from even thinking about it.

In the midst of the splendor, the habit of my tenacious ordinary mind asserted itself and I became afraid that the outer world had receded from me forever. Because I believed so completely in the physical world, and because I trusted it more than I trusted the light, I wanted to be reassured that it was still there, that I could see the crescent moon in the sky again, the splendid altar filled with candles, and the beautiful golden face of the lama.

But what would have been so terrible if I had stayed there in that brilliant green light awhile longer, if I had had more openness and trust, if I had been more willing? Later, one thinks this way. One notices the fear, the attachment to what seems solid, how one prefers the ordinary, how one rushes to grasp onto it again.

Over the years, I have mused about how the fierce being danced above the woman's abdomen and how those planes of green radiance appeared and filled all of space when everyone laughed. It is a bit odd to write all these experiences up in one recitation, unwrapping them like beautiful ornaments carefully taken out of the big fragrant containers of sawdust and wood shavings that were the rest of life-- workdays, friends, my daughter, lovers, the house shared with the Jewish renewal couple, the house shared with the poet who was a lousy housekeeper, or the house shared with the Japanese woman who sang at the window with her tamboura early each morning. But that is of course how they occurred, in the midst of the wood shavings, the miso soup, the children's homework, cutting up the cabbage.

One night I dreamed that I was a dolphin swimming through the air in a big, high-ceilinged room where Tarthang Tulku Rinpoche played with a sphere of mercury. I turned and leaped, while he threw the ball of mercury up into the air. Then with his mind he radiated the mercury into millions of brilliant shimmering patterns like fireworks, fountains, cascading waterfalls, evocative, beautiful, dissolving almost as soon as they appeared. From time to time he drew the mercury back into one sphere, where he let it hover in the air near his shoulder or hand. Then he scattered it again, and it created one scintillating pattern after the next.

While I swam, he spoke about the alchemical qualities of mercury. It had been used for centuries not only by Western alchemists, but in Tibet as well, he said. It was not necessarily a poisonous substance, it could be used. In order to master mercury, he said, one had to train the mind through meditation practice. Then, things that ordinary people thought of as magic might appear as a natural side-effect.

"Like right now," he said, looking at me. "You have changed into a dolphin." It was true, and I found the lama's statement completely delightful. Swerved and leaping through the air, I felt bliss and a profound sense of freedom.

Not long after, I had another dream that took place in that same large, high-ceilinged room. In the second dream, I was invisible, an observer placed up near the ceiling. Below, four beings composed more of vibrating light molecules than of any solid matter were performing a ritual dance. Their faces were fierce and beautiful. Their hair flowed upward in crackling flames. Their bodies radiated blazing light. Their movements were slow, like the movements of celestial bodies. Each movement of their eyes, each of their slow dance gestures was permeated with ecstatic knowing. In the grace of their slow turning and leaping, time and space fell away. Those beautiful dreams and the experience of the brilliant and pervasive green radiance still seem like wonderful blessings to me.

Spiritual teachings come in different forms and not all of them are comfortable. That's a bit of an understatement. In my experience, they are often uncomfortable. I had another opportunity to learn about that one Christmas Eve when I was hitchhiking, trying to get back to Bolinas from Berkeley. It was near dusk, and I carried two shopping bags full of presents for my daughter Danielle.

I had my thumb out; a car slowed and stopped. My first impression of the driver, a dark haired man, was ominous. Something told me, "Watch out. Look, his eyes are completely blank." There was a small dog in the back seat with one of its front legs in a splint. Another thought washed over the first, covering it. I observed, "He takes care of his dog. He must be okay." I dismissed my first impression and I climbed into the front seat of the car.

The man did not smile. What passed for a smile on his face was more like a twitch, as if laughter lived somewhere so far away, it was hard to recall it. Something was not good. My first impression was right. I began searching for clues and messages. He asked me where I was going, and I told him. Strange. After that, he said nothing. He never said, "I'll take you there, or I can only take you so far." He was silent, completely withdrawn.

I was afraid. I knew I had to engage him, so that he would reveal himself more. I don't know why this idea occurred to me but I began to consider the possibility that perhaps this man was actually Tarthang Tulku Rinpoche in disguise. Maybe he was trying to give me a spiritual test, to see if I could maintain pure view no matter what experience presented itself to me. If this man wasn't the lama, I thought, then certainly he was a teacher of some kind. He had the enlightened nature, just as every sentient being does.

I decided to look at him as an enlightened being in disguise while I continued to engage him in an ordinary way.

"Where are *you* going?" I asked in my most friendly, ingenuous manner. Then for the first time he turned his head fully toward me. The opaque cloths that covered his blank eyes lifted for a moment and I saw what lay beneath. His mouth opened. I felt his breath. "I'm going to the bondage house," he said, now quite wild with excitement. "Do you know what that is?" he asked, eyes wide. I wanted to burst out laughing. O ye gods, he suggests the bondage house. It was sardonically funny in its terrible sadness. Did I know what the bondage house was? Did I ever. At that moment, recollecting how my particular version of imprisonment had begun long before this strange man ever appeared in my life, I was even more sure that he was my spiritual teacher in disguise and that our meeting was a test of some kind.

Everything was pulsing. His face seemed to be in a strobe light. One moment the opaque eyes, the coarse mouth, the evil intention. The next moment, the peaceful, shining face of the lama. Back and forth, back and forth, he showed himself to me. I gathered my wits. Even if he was my teacher, I still had to deal with our encounter.

"I know the bondage house very well," I replied, surprised at how calm I felt. "And I am not going there any more. I am not going there with you." There. I had said it. It was final. Final and quite definite. He seemed shocked by my certainty. His fierce facade shrank down, and I could see the fear and grief move in waves beneath the surface of his aggression. But then he gathered his forces again and snarled. Grabbing the scarf around my neck, he tried to strangle me, feel my breast and drive at the same time. It wasn't workable. And I had the gift of calm. The experience, both very frightening and also very unreal, took place in another dimension as both a troubling human violation and a spiritual encounter.

I looked into his eyes. "Stop the car. I'm getting out," I told him firmly. He loosened his grip on my scarf and a bewildered look came over his face. Then, remembering his own mission, he sped up the car. I opened the door, determined to get out before we reached the freeway. "Don't!" he shouted, sounding at that moment like a small boy. "You'll hurt yourself!" I shook my head and laughed, amazed at the amount of energy coursing through my body. "You're worried about me hurting myself? That's strange. Just stop the car right now." He was deflated. His dark magic was dismantled and his illusory game dissolved, for the moment at least. He pulled the car over to the curb. I got out, taking the time to retrieve my shopping bags full of gifts. The opaque cloths were over his eyes. He would not look at me.

On the sidewalk, I watched him drive away. Then my legs began to shake and my teeth chattered. I could not get his license plate, even though I thought I should have tried. My mind was scattered. Maybe he really was the teacher in disguise. Maybe he was just a man intent on his distorted passions. I don't know if our encounter touched his heart in any way, if he remembered my eyes as I saw the teacher in him. I know that viewing him as a teacher saved me because it gave me the courage to cut through conventional reactions. If he came to test me, I am thankful for the exercise. Since the whole thing was essentially without inherent existence, I eventually released it. And being a smart woman, I didn't hitchhike after that, either.

Chapter 4 Reborn Again

"Sharp nostalgia, infinite and terrible, for what I already possess."

--JUAN RAMON JIMENEZ

Everything can be killed except nostalgia for the kingdom, we carry it in the color of our eyes, in every love affair, in everything that deeply torments and unties and tricks."

--JULIO CORTAZAR

ONE BRIGHT, SUNNY AFTERNOON I WAS sitting in the front room of a Victorian house, one of a bevy of beautiful old houses near San Francisco's Golden Gate Park. This particular house was the headquarters of Theta Institute, where rebirthing, a newly developed technique for healing birth trauma, was being pioneered. I had been interviewing people there about rebirthing for five days. Now I was going to get rebirthed myself and photographer Sandy Solomon would chronicle the whole thing for *New Age Journal*, an exciting new magazine focused on healing, personal growth and social change.

The idea of getting photographed during my rebirthing experience didn't seem strange to me at the time. It was the Seventies, the era of what my friend Ponderosa Pine liked to call *radical disclosure*. While I waited for Sandy to arrive, I gazed at the New Age sayings posted on the walls. I don't recall exactly what they said, but I do remember thinking, "Oh yeah, right" in a sarcastic way. I was doing my best to be more vulnerable and open, as befits a Californian, but I still thought like a New Yorker and I knew it.

I was ready to be rebirthed because I was weary of how difficult life could be. ..."still so completely chained and fettered by my sins and my attachments," as Thomas Merton once said of himself. I doubt that I thought of it this way then, as if my difficulty was my own problem. I was still in the habit of blaming the outside world for my various habitual reactions, faux pas and peccadillos. The way I looked at things, all I was trying to do was find my so-called self and wrest some pleasure from life. Both occupations seemed innocent enough. But I was not always innocent.

That poor 30-year old gal, so brash and impulsive, so burdened with her personal history, appetites, dreams and ambitions. You can look at your earlier incarnations like this by the time you're in your seventies, because you've already lived a lot. In the process, you've hopefully healed some old wounds, fulfilled at least a passel of your dreams, refined your appetites and grown kinder than you were when you were younger.

Yes, there are days when I think, "Why the hell didn't I have more confidence and trust by the time I was 30? I would be in a different place than I am today if I had gotten the hang of life earlier." Maybe. Where I am today is the result of a lot of experimentation, mistakes, work and play. Can't change the past. It happened that way because that was what I called up, what I needed.

I am sitting here on a winter day thinking about how you can move thousands of miles away, change your name, profession or gender, but no matter how radically you re-invent yourself, it may just mean that you are shifting the hiding places for what really needs attention. That was often the case with me earlier in my life. I'm not saying that I'm completely cured of it either.

Back to my rebirthing story. I found some of the slogans on the walls of the sitting room annoying. But overall they were less obnoxious than the walls themselves, which were the color of cooked liver. Not an appealing color, no matter what you say. Even if you find the color lavender irritating, at least you know where you stand. But those liver-colored walls gave me the creeps. After all, I was there for a rather intimate procedure. When you are about to put your psyche and your physical body alike into the hands of strangers, you prefer that the walls not be painted the color of the liver or any other internal organs. I felt they were lacking in empathy. They could have just painted the room off white.

No matter color what the walls had been, I would have been nervous. Perhaps I was brave, all things considered. It's not every day that one confronts one's birth. And that's what I was about to do in that big building, in some room underneath the rich red carpeting. I had no idea what it meant.

Sandy arrived with her camera, and one of the rebirthers appeared to greet us. We talked about the house philosophy, which included not just healing the birth trauma with rebirthing, but attracting prosperity and moving towards immortality. I was wondering about the immortality business. Why would a person want to live forever? The rebirther sighed repeatedly as we conversed. I learned later that sighing was part of the culture at Theta Institute. Sighing, he told me, was a breathing release they considered essential to moving energy. Even after he explained it, it seemed like a rather dispirited way of expressing yourself, maybe even another bad sign. I could have decided to stop right there. I certainly considered it because I was afraid of what might happen. But my curiosity overcame my fear and we headed downstairs where I took off my clothes and climbed into the hot tub loaded down with the assorted emotional freight and habits accumulated from over three decades of living.

At first, I had to become familiar with the snorkel and the noseplug. But there was something else and it was far more demanding than technical adjustment. I had to surrender to the guidance and help of the two rebirthers as they supported my body in the warm water. I had at least as many impressions and opinions about them as I had about anyone else. Which of course included judgments, criticisms and fears. The whole business swept through my mind as we began.

It really was the story of the color of the living room all over again. What color could possibly reassure me? What sort of person could possibly make me feel completely safe? They seemed kind. But they were *only human*-- as we are fond of saying about each other. Perhaps they were really waiting to drown me. Finally, I had to laugh at myself and let go. I chose to trust them and the situation, which I had set up myself, after all.

My body felt so quiet in the water as the two of them supported me at the hips. My arms seemed very long, trailing like pieces of kelp. I began to lose a sense of connection with my body. I kept trying to come back to it, but it seemed such hard work and gradually I let it go. Then it seemed that I was traveling deep into some dark landscape. Images went away. Colors went away. I heard only the sound of my own breathing. It was inside me. It filled me. There was nothing but breath. The physical world dissipated and expanded into other dimensions. The dark night of water was filled with sound, breath taken in and breath let out. We could have been there for thousands of years. I lost track of time, direction and body.

A sound brought me tenuously back into my body, or brought my body back around my breath. From deep inside the internal landscape, I heard a baby crying. Its wail was terribly painful—it sounded so alone, abandoned, helpless, confused and afraid. I don't know what my body was doing, whether I was thrashing or lying still. I only know that the baby's cry awakened me from an oceanic dream. That poor baby's suffering was unbearable. I wanted to take care of it, but its pain was so vast, as if the pain of the entire world was captured within its tiny body.

Then, a second sound appeared. A deep sound--centered, peaceful, ancient. It arose from the base of my spine and traveled up to my crown in a golden radiance. Both sounds were within me. The difference between the crying baby and the deep golden sound made my tongue grow thick. Panic swept through me. Suffocation. The feeling of drowning.

"Yes, let's take her out of the tub now. She needs to rest," I heard one of the rebirthers say to the other. I couldn't make any response. I was pinned somewhere far within myself experiencing the contrast between the powerless pain of the baby and the deep peace of the golden sound.

They wrapped me in a soft blanket and placed me on a flat surface, touching me gently. My hands constricted, my face paralyzed, I was bursting with pain and grief. With growing surprise and shock, I realized that I was the baby who was about to be born. "Keep breathing," the two rebirthers said over and over as they bent over me, massaging my arms and legs. It was difficult to remember breathing in the tornado of panic that engulfed me. Perhaps I did not want to breathe. Perhaps it would be better not to breathe, not to emerge into air.

Slippery dark constrictions pressed my heart, feelings with no name. It seemed so hard. I was afraid to live. Then I heard myself yelling out loud. "Let me go! Let me go! Let me go!" My eyes were closed but I was looking at my mother. She seemed surprised, as if she hadn't even realized that she was holding me back. I felt a surge of love and compassion for her, for both of us, caught together in the wild confusion of human life. After awhile, my hands began to unclench and

175

my jaw relaxed. My body pulsed with energy; I lay there half in and half out of this world. In front of me, I saw a luminous spiral of beings in the sky, beautiful as angels, their transparent bodies radiating rays of rainbow colors. I saw that they were mothers and daughters, generation after generation giving birth and being born. Then an image of Avalokiteshvara, the Buddha of compassion, appeared in front of me. His eyes looked into mine. These appearances invigorated and comforted me, drawing me as they did into the deep song, the immaterial resonant net of which the world is made.

Surrendering into the waters of the unconscious and the hands of strangers that day, I had a glimpse of both the profound pain and the majestic splendor immanent in everything. It made me feel profoundly grateful to be alive. And that feeling was not one I had a lot of experience with up until then.

As a child of 10 or 11 I often woke in the morning with a feeling of dread thinking of the effort it would take to ford the river of the day. There was a sheaf of unspoken sorrows I couldn't dislodge stuffed in my throat where my voice should have been and they greeted me each morning, giving me a nauseous feeling. I thought I was a special case, the only person in exile, the only one separated from her real tribe, disconnected from Nature, floating in a strange laboratory experiment called New Jersey suburbs.

It seemed that the other people around me fit in better or accepted the situation more easily. I don't know whether they really accepted it or not. Perhaps they also had their own existential discontents. I imagine they did. Of course they did. And because these kinds of difficulties arrive as part of the experience of isolation or separation, they probably thought they were the only ones suffering from that particular brand of pain, too.

By the time I reached California, I was determined to live out in the open. I knew that meant healing the wounds of childhood. And wasn't I in the right place to do that, having landed in The Golden State, where every form of healing and spiritual hoo-ha was in full force?

My first contact with the world of healing happened at the Headlands Healing Service in Bolinas, where an osteopath named Dr. Irving Oyle was engaged in a pioneering investigation into how mind affects well-being, which believe it or not was a very innovative idea at the time. Oyle and his methods were controversial. He wasn't like a regular doctor, people said, and that was certainly true. First of all, he had no standard fees, treating patients with an apparent disregard for monetary compensation. Some people found this suspicious. Besides that, he often asked those who came to see him, "Why did you allow yourself to become ill?" as a way of encouraging people to look underneath the surface of their symptoms into the deeper causes of their malaise. But many of his patients just wanted pills and found the question annoying or irrelevant.

I didn't know anything then about Oyle's life story-- his work with Bread and Puppet Theater in New York or how a journey he took to treat cave-dwelling Indians in Mexico changed the course of his life as a physician. I didn't know that he was friends with Stanley Krippner, Director of the Dream Laboratory of Maimonides Hospital in New York or that he had treated counter-culture hero Abbie Hoffman, who in 1969 published an article about Oyle in the Los Angeles Free Press titled *Doctors Join the Revolution*. "I write this lying in a hospital bed during my third week of hepatitis," Hoffman wrote. "When the disease first hit me I went to see Dr. Irving Oyle. A rarity in the world of medicine, he is totally dedicated to curing patients and doesn't give a shit about money. A few years ago he was running a successful practice out on Long Island with the right kind of patients. Somehow it wasn't giving him the kind of gratification he wanted, so he closed up shop and headed for the ghetto in New York's lower East Side. As for practicing medicine, the lower East Side must seem more like the Wild West. Firmly entrenched in a storefront office that one could easily mistake for one of the Motherfucker dens, he carries on a lone struggle to bring medical care to an area that could use fifty to one hundred Dr. Oyles."

All I knew about Oyle was that he was a balding, not at all sexy middle-aged man with a wife and family, and that he was into healing, a subject about which I was completely uninformed. I knew a lot about hiding, and was also proficient at burying the evidence of my crimes at least most of the time, but healing had never been part of my world.

Even so, healing had already begun. Whales had appeared in answer to my prayer and I had played music for the Tibetan lama while the room vibrated, dissolved and coalesced again. So I began to study creative visualization at the Headlands Healing Service, which was tucked away in a room of the old white Presbyterian Church in downtown Bolinas. The Shoshone medicine man Rolling Thunder appeared at Headlands one day, causing quite a stir in town.

A medicine man is supposed to have a direct conduit to the healing energies of the cosmos. Rolling Thunder looked around at the group of us creative visualizers, which included some young doctors that were apprenticing with Irving, some healers and healer wannabes. Rolling Thunder took our measure with his penetrating eyes. We were seriously looked at. That in itself was the most noteworthy part of his visit to me. Nothing else sticks in my memory.

We increased our ability to visualize by gazing at images on the wall, then closing our eyes and looking at the images again. I seem to remember an image of a watermelon slice. I'm certain that there were many other images, but I do not recall any of them. Perhaps if I sat here for awhile and brought back that room and that time, more of them would re-appear. I've done that with other memories. But I don't really care that much about unearthing the rest of the pictures that hung high up on the wall in our visualization class.

Dr. Irving Oyle assured us that there was an innate healing power within everyone. He believed that each person should take responsibility for their health, and in the process look deeply into the sources of their imbalances, rather than relying only upon quick fix medicine. These ideas have become mainstream now, but at the time, they were revolutionary, even in the far-out little village of Bolinas.

Irving had great faith in the power of community involvement in personal healing. Rather than shipping people off to the psychiatric ward at Two North when they had bad drug reactions from some hallucinogen, Irving suggested that we first do our best to help people on bad trips within the community. I was part of one such circle, hastily called-together to help a thin blond woman whose acid trip had gone bad. She moved erratically around the room like a frightened, injured creature. She didn't seem to know where she was. It was clear that she didn't trust us. In this kind of situation, Irving was completely calm and at ease. No strange expression or behavior seemed to faze him. His confidence encouraged the rest of us to relax and after a few hours, we gradually brought the woman back, using the power of our group intention, our words, and our love.

Oyle could be inspirational, but he was also confrontational. I often found his blunt manner annoying and avoided seeing him as a physician until one day when I found myself in considerable pain. The muscles in my lower back had seized up; the pain was wearing me down. My back had been going out that way every few months. Usually, I dealt with it by wearing a back brace. I thought that ignoring it or toughing it out was my best option. Such was my stalwart approach to all sorts of pain.

My father had similar episodes with his back. They usually occurred after he was coming off a drinking binge. He would wind up immobilized on the floor of some room in the house, with my mother applying compresses to his clenched muscles. It was almost as if he had to undergo some kind of punishment, like being hit with divine retribution. Perhaps when my own back went out, I regarded it in a similar way, as punishment for my excesses. But if I did have that notion, I was not conscious of it because in those days I was out of touch with the relationship between my body, emotions and spirit.

So I was driven by the back pain to see Irving Oyle as a doctor. After some examination and discussion, he looked me in the eye and said in his usual blunt way, "I know you are not going to like this, but your back pain comes from anger." My reaction to his statement was both funny and quite predictable, considering who I was then. I became really angry.

"That's just ridiculous," I yelled at him. "What kind of a stupid doctor are you? I come here in terrible pain and all you do is tell me I made it happen because I am angry? Screw you, Irving." How irritating he was. What a terrible doctor.

He just sat there and laughed. I took off, fuming, thinking what a jerk he was and he hadn't even given me any medicine. I had just as much pain when I left as I did when I went in. I didn't want to hear any of his views, which were complete bullshit, as far as I was concerned. I had no wish to investigate the source of my back pain. I was too busy running away.

He really did give me quite a useful treatment that day, though I certainly had no appreciation for it at the time. Thanks to his provocation, I began to cast furtive glances at the possibility that my emotions might have something to do with my back spasms. I paid more attention to what was going on mentally and emotionally each time my back went out. After some time went by, I realized that Oyle was right. Now every time I think of that appointment, I chuckle and send up a little hallelujah to him. Wonderful, annoying Irving Oyle. I guess he was what the Universe thought I needed as an introduction to the vast territory of healing.

Healing has been a keen interest and occupation of mine since then. I've studied and practiced many forms of spiritual and natural healing including laying on of hands, distant healing, sound healing, rapid eye healing and hypnotherapy. Over the years, I have become quite aware of the healing power of thought, emotion, laughter, diet, movement, voice, touch-- and last but not least the healing power of stillness, of simply resting in the natural mind.

Healing is a big subject. Maybe it's the only subject. Healing as in returning to an innate experience of wholeness, connecting with larger forces and energies, understanding and accepting oneself and one's life, expanding one's understanding of what is real. Healing can take the form of a spiritual epiphany, or losing oneself in ecstatic lovemaking. We can find healing in the tall grasses and in the sand, in sacred initiation and blessing. Healing brings us back. We remember who we are essentially, beyond the particulars of personality, history and habit.

Healing can blind us like bright sunlight, opening our eyes in new ways until we feel the warm, astounding magnificence of what is. Healing brings us back to original grace. There are many roads, many bright flashes, and because healing is not always easy, many trials, labyrinths and dark caves along the way. It's inevitable that when I think about healing, I come to recall some of my trips on LSD, especially my first trip. I was in my late 20s. It was the summer that I lived in Provincetown and longed for the deathless love of the wonderful Italian painter Al di Lauro. But that is a story for another day.

When I dropped the LSD I intended to be alone. I wanted the time and space to take a look at my mind. I hadn't ever really trusted my mind and I thought it was time to shift that. If I can't trust my own mind, I thought, what can I trust? What was it that I was trying to trust? My thoughts, my sensations, my intuition? I didn't have it broken down. In talking with myself about it, I just said, well, here we are, mind. Let's get to know each other better.

No matter how many jokes may accumulate about psychedelics, I'm in favor of acknowledging the powerful and amazing experience that they can unlock. Between the years 1967 and 1972 studies with terminal cancer patients showed that LSD combined with psychotherapy could alleviate symptoms of depression, tension, anxiety, sleep disturbances, psychological withdrawal, and even severe physical pain that was resistant to opiates.

Last year an article in the New York Times reported how the use of psychedelics among the terminally ill eased their fear of dying.

"I now have the distinct sense that there's so much more," said one woman who took psylicibum in a recent study, "so many different states of being. I have the sense that death is not the end but just part of a process, a way of moving into a different sphere, a different way of being."

If psychedelics can be so helpful to the dying, can't they also be helpful to the living? I ask you. You can probably guess my own answer to the question.

I dropped the acid sitting by myself in my rented cottage. The first thing I discovered is just how fascinating wallpaper can be. Its ordinary pattern became animated, permutating and dancing, radiating light, metamorphosing ornately, like some kind of hieroglyphic asking to be understood. I gazed at the wallpaper for what seemed a very, very long time. Finally I had had enough of its marvels.

I walked from the living room to the bathroom, a journey that took a great deal of time and energy. I wanted to look at myself in the mirror. That old question, "Who am I?" was lurking nearby. What better time to ask it than when in the midst of a psychedelic experience? Gazing at my face, I saw it as a somewhat unfamiliar assortment of features that were far from fixed. My face reminded me of some of Picasso's paintings. The right eye leapt out, then subsided. The nose moved here and there, the mouth changed color and shape. I wasn't accustomed to my face metamorphosing that way. Metamorphosing is such a big word for it though.

My face was shifting and moving fast. Many faces were blurring one into another like balls being juggled by a cosmic joker. I couldn't keep track of it. Where was my face, the face I thought was mine? Did I have a face, or was it something I made up? What was this rapid stream of countless faces displaying themselves one after the next?

Occasionally I saw only darkness, no faces at all. It was disconcerting, but I am a basically curious person, so I kept looking in the mirror at the myriads of faces that poured through. Who were those beings, many of whom seemed vulgar or even barbaric? Did they live within me? Were they an expression of my past lives? Were they infinite, or was there an end to them? When my familiar face showed itself for a moment, I remembered the question that had led me to look in the mirror originally. "Who am I?" You are permeable and interconnected with everything, the mirror seemed to say.

I walked out into the night and stood under the dark vault of heaven, which was beautiful and vast, bejeweled with stars set in gorgeous patterns like an ancient mystery I still did not understand. The moonlight was liquid silver on the bay, on the boats, on the road. In the immense darkness the moonlight was cool and healing and I was one tiny part of it all.

I feel fortunate because my journey has been blessed with beautiful insights, coincidences and initiations, even though I have lived all my life in a culture that ignores the real rites of passage.

On the day that Tarthang Tulku built a big altar in the parking lot to celebrate Buddha's birthday, my friend Toni rushed up to me excitedly and whispered, "Rinpoche said there will be some initiations today! What do you think that means?" I agreed that it was thrilling that initiations might be part of the program, but of course, neither of us had any idea what the lama had in mind. Was the experience of radiant emerald light that filled me when he suggested that everyone give a big laugh part of his initiatory plan?

And before then, what about the day when the blackbird flew into the house when I asked the question, "Why did I take that Blackbird name anyway?" And the day Magda came to visit and then when she left, how the ancient voice came through me with the brilliant column of white light? What about the whales answering my prayers? And long before that, when I was a child, why did my secret friend the mountain hermit and my challenger the dark monster appear?

I have turned these memories over and over in my mind. I no longer care about finding explanations for those peculiar events, but I do treasure them as talismans of the deep song. I have been surprised, disordered and expanded in spontaneous, coincidental initiations.

The story is not over yet. Dying is sure to be a glorious initiation. And there may well be a few more spontaneous surprises in store before death appears.

I've been reviewing the events, patterns and themes of my life for 17 years. Nowadays in the field of aging they call this process life review or reminiscence. According to Jung, it is one of the important tasks of aging. A person wants to make sense of her experience. Even so, many people have never heard of the value of life review as a spiritual practice, a method for finding meaning, for resolving difficult aspects of the past and for detaching from one's experience in preparation for dying. In the broader culture, you hear people use the phrase "living in the past" as a condescending put-down for some old person's absorption in what was. There are good reasons why older people spend time reviewing the past. We have much more of a past than a future for one thing. We are already setting sail for the next part of our journey and so we live halfway in this world and halfway in the next world, however you think of that. I suppose there is a difference between living in the past and life review though. Even though I contemplate the past, I don't live in it. I do my best to live in the present in a vivid way, which my friend Marian VanEyk McCain who wrote the book Elderwoman calls *radical aliveness.* This part of life is powerful. Powerful--that's not something our society associates with aging. Too bad. I hope that changes, and soon. It takes decades to become oneself and to refine one's skills and gifts. By the time a person is old, she has her entire life experience to offer, and wants to offer it. She does not want to be ignored or cast off as if she is an outdated appliance of some kind.

Two older people I met while I was still in my 30s had a lasting influence on my life. It's only now that I am old myself that I begin to understand what part their age played in my relationship to them and their own relationship to the world. Both of them were deeply comfortable with themselves and their life work. Both were generous, altruistic, loving and strong. Both were devoted to a noble mission. I'll tell you about Richard St. Barbe-Baker first.

From childhood on, I've had a deep yearning to live in the midst of profusely untrammeled, riotously beautiful Nature. I think it was this yearning for the Garden that led me to Richard St. Barbe Baker, a deeply spiritual man who spent his life preserving and reclaiming forests all over the world. I heard about St. Barbe from Carolyn Schafer, a friend at the San Francisco Ecology Center who had just returned from Findhorn, a spiritual community in Scotland. As soon as I heard her speak about St. Barbe, I knew I had to meet him. I got his address from her. I wrote to him, pouring out in that first letter my concerns for Earth and the future of the creatures that inhabit it. He wrote back in an elegant, old-fashioned script. With that, our friendship began. It lasted for seven years, a short time in linear reckoning. But according to the more chaotic and expansive measuring that goes on within the psyche, it is a meeting that still augments me.

Less than a year after our first exchange of letters, I received a call from a woman who was a follower of the Bahai faith. St. Barbe, who was a Bahai, was coming to speak to a small group at her home. She was calling because he wanted to invite me to join them. That's how I found myself in a modest living room in a town south of San Francisco with about 25 Bahai believers, most of whom had never met St. Barbe either. We mingled for awhile. Then St. Barbe Baker entered the room. He was slightly heavy and a little stooped with age. His hair and his mustache were pure white, his eyes clear and mild. With his ruddy cheeks and comfortable tweedy clothing, he was the picture of an old English gentleman who loves being outdoors. Walking slowly across the room, he surveyed us with a gentle gaze. When he reached the wing chair where he would sit, he lowered himself slowly into it. At the same time, his eyes connected with each person in the room. "Help me," he said simply as he eased his old body into the chair. Help me!

I was riveted and a bit afraid. This "help me" of St. Barbe's went far beyond my usual horizon. I lacked his calm joy, the depth and breadth of his commitment to great forests and to the nurturing, enriching quality of what he called "Earth's living green mantle." St. Barbe saw Nature as a divine display and the restoration of forests as an act of prayer. His dedication to the presence of forests was a metaphysical pledge. Calling us to help him, he conjured up in us the Garden with its deep, booming resonance, a wordless language that beats through our cells carrying the memory of Earth wisdom from long ages ago.

My heart and imagination were stirred as he talked. I could feel the trees shaking their branches. I heard the papery leaves of the birch and aspen, the rustle of long-needled pine, the ancient gingko, the rowan with its red berries, giant redwoods and cedars, the willow, apple, pear, plum, the cherry trailing its petals like a veil on the spring wind, the lombardy poplar, the columnar cypress and the mighty oak, the juniper, spruce, olive, the locust, the sycamore. I felt them brushing against me, and the freshness of their scents and juicy sap, flowers and fruits, their cool leaves, comforting bark, slender trunks, gigantic girth, and even their roots were dancing.

I think the trees whirled me round and round because for a brief moment or two I found myself in old Middle Earth in the company of Ents, those ancient tree-like beings Tolkein wrote about, who carry the ancestral memory of trees and of the Earth itself. Did St. Barbe know he had led us into sacred groves where trees old beyond our paltry analysis and reckoning emerged? As he spoke, the immense Ents emerged from hiding places deep in great forests and moved slowly through the landscape. Along the way, mute, disem-powered trees and animals drank in their booming rever-beration, remembering ways of being from which they had long been isolated. We humans absorbed the Entish vibra-tion too, feeling it in our flesh and minds, a shimmer recon-necting circuitry we had forgotten. Things opened out and brightened; the dissonance faded-- of Moloch and Mordor the memory loosened. The Hackensacks, tarpaper shacks, living in cars and under freeways lightened and grew thin, and the experience of the primordial Garden brightened. All this came from his simple plea for help as he sat both vivid and worn from the accumulation of his years. Tears welled in my eyes. If only more men were like him. Many more. And women, too. Then we would not have arrived at this place of global desolation that the deluded describe as progress.

Later that evening St. Barbe sat with me. I was touched by the way he gathered me in like an old friend. He described the weeks he once spent in a coma, how outwardly he had been close to death but inwardly, he found himself back in the Garden. Every variety of tree grew there he said; the air was filled with the perfume of their flowers and fruit, and the scent of their leaves and needles and bark. In the very middle of The Garden, he told me, the immense World Tree towered, beautifully ornamented with the symbols of the world's religions, with four rivers coming out of it in the four directions. St. Barbe spent weeks in a coma, wandering delightedly through the leafy allees of The Garden. He did not want to return to earthly life, he said, but was told he had to come back. So he followed that instruction and lived out his life as a planetary forester.

Much about St. Barbe was like my own father, who loved Nature and the invisible world of spirit with a passion that he communicated to me on walks through the woods and along the coastline of New Jersey. My dear father and I mused over stones, leaves, earth, insects and fish.

We pondered the mysteries of clouds, earth and water, the dancing course of fireflies in the summer night, the dancing course of snowflakes in the winter days. But when I returned later to walk again in the wooded areas we frequented during my childhood, how small and cramped they seemed! How worn and used, especially the place around Garrett Mountain, which was more of a hill really, where the fabulous Catholina Lambert had built a large stone castle in the style of Medieval Revival right there by Paterson, New Jersey.

To me the place, which had been deserted for years, seemed dismal. Why, I had always wondered when I was a child, why had he made such a dank, lightless dwelling for himself and his wife? I puzzled over it. Perhaps I missed what it had meant to Lambert, now that he was no longer there to speak for it. He may have hung long banners on its walls, and kept merry fires burning, and perhaps his walks in those woods refreshed his soul. He could have been like me, a person in flight from New Jersey. He might have built the castle as a refuge from it, or a transport into another world in the midst of it.

Whatever his castle and its grounds were for him, those woods were a magical playground to my father and me. In my childhood, they seemed to extend far and wide. Each lichen and fern took up an entire universe of space and thought. The groves of trees were immense, fragrant and deep. All its little spiders and their webs, the smell of pine needles and moldy leaves, its berries and flowers gave me joy and delight. When my father took me there one night so that I could see the constellations whirling in the sky, I wanted to fly up into the air and never return to our flat, to the tidy boxwood hedges of our neighborhood, and certainly not to the inscrutable dilemmas of adults.

Because adults did have inscrutable dilemmas, if my father was any example. He often sat in his armchair poring over metaphysical matters as described in the Rosacrucian Magazine. The cover of that magazine was so different from the covers of other magazines in our household. It depicted no happy homemakers wearing aprons, no fly fishermen in the middle of a rushing stream. Instead, there was a beatific person of no discernable gender wearing a long white robe, a person who stood on a high mountaintop, arms raised up as if rejoicing. I liked that picture. When I turn the eyes of my imagination to my father, I notice the quality of his concentration as he reads. There is something wonderful about it. It brings out his best qualities and makes me remember how much I loved him and how much he taught me. Reading the Rosacrucian Magazine, my father shed the dust of his everyday struggle and he was at ease.

He also careened off and disappeared into the dark, smelly interior of taverns and emerged many hours later, another man entirely. I grieved for many years over his sorrow and confusion, his drinking, guilt and unlived dreams and felt bereaved by the shame and isolation of his drinking. Yet I do not wish to presume that I understand my father's life any more than I wish to presume I understand the life of the legendary Lambert of Garrett Mountain. I may know something, but I do not know enough. All I can really say about it is this. I loved my father enormously, deeply, intensely. I am happy for the love we shared, grateful that we both loved Nature and spirit. I do not know if I saw my father's noble aspects and kingly potential more than he did himself. But see it I did, and something in me insisted that he enter the domain of his brightness. When instead year after year he chose furtively to slip ever further away despite my prayers and inner seething, I repudiated him as if he were an apostate of his own true religion. I excommunicated him. I told him I wouldn't speak with him again unless he stopped drinking.

For the last three years of my father's life, we were estranged. And I, newly removed to California's golden shores, did not conceive of his mortality or imagine that my father might die before we had resolved our rift. Perhaps we would not have healed it, but we would have set it aside and taken the opportunity to rest in the love we shared with each other. That did not happen. Instead, my father had a heart attack on a street in Paterson, New Jersey and died. My dear father who wound up living in a room at the YMCA lay dead in the street. Someone even stole his ring from his dead hand.

I received a call. Who was it from? My mother? My brother? I don't remember. It was a foggy day in Bolinas. The cypresses and eucalyptus trees appeared and disappeared in whiteness. My heart was breaking that November day. I got into my car and drove off into the fog, out Mesa Road to the abalone beaches. There was no one on the road all the way. How could there be anyone anywhere? The world was utterly emptied of life, of meaning. I drove in dumb desolation, with the landscape shrouded in fog and the pulse of my father booming in me like thunder.

I thought of driving my car off one of the high cliffs of the headlands. I would plummet in whiteness until my grief was drowned in the sea. Instead I unwittingly drove off the steep end of a tricky road I never navigated before. The car landed nearly perpendicular in the dirt, about eight feet down. It was clear that I could go no further. I had to sit and look at the dark leafy earth in front of my windshield, the same dark earth that would receive my dear father's body. I had to contemplate again from a far more radical perspective questions that had haunted me before. How could it be that my father and I who loved each other so much had remained so isolate? How could it be that my father in whose heart bloomed such rich gardens of inquiry had withered and dwindled so basely? And how in the world could it be that my dear father lived in the Y like a friendless man, and died on the street alone? It was unbearable.

> *"I will not see it!*
> *No chalice can contain it,*
> *no swallows can drink it,*
> *no frost of light can cool it,*
> *nor song nor deluge of white lilies,*
> *no glass can cover it with silver,*
> *No.*
> *I will not see it!"*
>
> ---Federico Garcia Lorca,
> Lament for Ignacio Sanchez Mejias

Several months after my father died, I had a dream. In it, my father was lying in a coffin. "What have you done to him?" I yelled out, though nobody was there. "What have you done to him?" I wanted to blame someone for his death. Then the coffin was in my hand like a tiny talisman. I held it and thought of my father--the bouncing pony rides on his knees, the way he dramatically sang *O Cichonya,* fishing with him for bluefish in the bay, his reeling, apologetic drunks.

Suddenly, he appeared right next to me and we were talking. "How are you?" I asked, well aware that he was no longer in the body he appeared to have around him. "Fine," he said. He did seem well. His vest and jacket had many pockets. He began going through each of them, looking for something. "I wanted to talk to you because we didn't have a chance before, and I wanted to ask you about something." Finally, he fished out two tickets and showed them to me. He looked hopeful, as if he suspected that I could give him some clue about them. They were two tickets to The Black Crown Ceremony, a ceremony given by His Holiness the Gyalwa Karmapa. I had attended two Black Crown ceremonies, both amazing and exalting events. "Do you know what these are?" he asked me. I nodded my head affirmatively. "Can we go together?" he asked with all the excitement of a small child. I gave a big sigh. I really felt very happy. "Yes, we can," I said to him. That dream eased my sorrow and regret. It was the start of forgiving him and myself.

I saw in St. Barbe my father's sensitivity and nobility. But in him they were undiminished by the conflict, shame and frustration that vied for my own father's life energies. The wonderful potentials that lived in my father as a small delicate plant were in St. Barbe flourishing fields and groves. What was it that made the difference between the life of my father and the life of St. Barbe? What made St. Barbe rise and expand into his life and my father twirl and dwindle? It is difficult to speak of my father this way. I do not wish to reduce him to his unmet challenges. Because in spite of every bitter betrayal, he was my beloved father, a dreamer who wished to wander in gypsy wagons, a philosopher who pondered the nature of God and the universe, a jovial presence whose silly songs and stories made us laugh uproariously, a gentle observer of the wave, the cloud, the butterfly, the caterpillar. When I think of my father now, I wonder what his life would have been if he had pushed through the bars of his personal hell by dedicating himself to some noble purpose, something much bigger than the sharp confines of his sorrow.

My father was fascinated with the metaphysical. He felt oneness with the divine in Nature and called himself a pantheist to indicate his sweep and acceptance. Yet I wonder if in all that abundant feast of pantheism he ever took much real spiritual sustenance, if he felt the divine within himself or if it always remained something outside of him. When he was drunk, he bedeviled himself as a worthless outcast. He loved to sing, *"We're poor little lambs who have lost our way, baaa, baaa, baaa. Little black sheep who have gone astray, baa, baaa, baaa. Gentlemen songsters off on a spree, doomed from here to eternity, Lord have pity on such as we, baaa, baaa, baaa."*

How I hated that song and his hapless, idiotic expression when he sang it. He chose to lose himself, to make a romance of his doomed adventures. From my vantage point, his adventures were not romantic but awful, embarrassing, deeply disturbing. I suppose it is inevitable that a person like me, with a darling, lovable, romantically doomed father such as I had, may be inclined to search for another kind of father, which I found in St. Barbe. After our initial meeting, our friendship continued in an exchange of letters. I don't know why he took the time to communicate with me and to support my efforts and my spirit. He was a busy and inspired man, someone whose work was internationally known. But then, love doesn't make any logical sense at all. From the first, our connection seemed as if it had existed for lifetimes. He saw into layers of my being that others never noticed.

St. Barbe, who had great respect and affinity for native peoples, asked me when we first met if I had native American blood. I told him, yes, I had a little. From then on he addressed me as "my Cherokee princess," a term of endearment that delighted me. "You are a great Earth-healer, my Cherokee princess," he wrote in one letter. "Never forget your work to heal the Earth." I don't know why he called me a great Earth-healer. I hope I am.

We corresponded for years. He was always traveling in his continued efforts to reforest the planet. I moved from working to save the whales into freelance environmental activism and journalism, and then into holistic healing and

Buddhist studies. His letters arrived from Canada, Israel and Africa. I no longer have any of those letters. I wish I did. But they have disappeared somewhere along the way; I am left with what I recall. That must be enough.

Finally the time came when one of my letters to him went unanswered. I wrote another and there was no response. For months a dull feeling of loss moved in me. But I was unsure whether St. Barbe was actually gone. One spring day the following year, my friend Katie said that she was going to visit some friends who lived near the Umpqua River. "There's an old man visiting them, and he is someone who has planted a lot of trees," she said. I became quite excited by her news. It had to be St. Barbe. It was! "I didn't know if he was still alive!" I exclaimed. "He is, but he is very ill," she said. A few days later we made a journey to the farm where St. Barbe was staying. I was overjoyed at the prospect of seeing him again.

When we arrived, he was sitting under a big tree talking with a group of people. He looked very weary and sick. Several minutes after we arrived, some people helped him back to his bed. I wondered whether he was too ill to see us. We sat down under the big trees and refreshed ourselves with some cool tea. About thirty minutes later, someone came out to say that St. Barbe would visit with us for a short time. We tiptoed in and sat around his bed. He said very little. A woman came in and suggested that it was time for us to leave. With a gesture, he asked me to stay on. I was deeply moved, as I had been that evening we first met in the gathering of Bahai believers. We sat looking at each other in silence. Without saying a word, I poured out my heart to him. He was like a mirror, or calm water. I could have sat there with him in that state of communion for a long time. I wanted to. I knew it would be the last time in this life. Each of us has to pass through the portals of death. St. Barbe's time was coming. I looked at his peaceful eyes and his long earlobes, which Buddhists believe are the sign of the Boddhisattva, and at his long, beautiful hands. I knew he felt my love in waves, as I felt his for me.

"I am going soon," he said finally. "I know," I responded. "I will return to Saskatchewan, where I began my work, and I will die there," he told me gently. "I am glad I have had the opportunity to see you again," I said. "I am glad to see you again, my Cherokee princess," he answered softly. He closed his eyes and we sat again in silence. Conversation seemed a bulky afterthought, compared to the silence. Everything we said in words had already been said in the stillness, and so much more that was subtle and non conceptual.

When St. Barbe opened his eyes again, he looked at me and said quietly, "But you have something you still want to say to me." It was true. "I think you already know this," I began. "But I want to tell you anyway. It seems important. Please, when you die, send your spiritual essence out through the crown of your head and merge with the light." We continued to gaze at each other. He had no visible response whatsoever. He did not speak or nod or give any indication of agreement. Why should he, I thought to myself. There was no need to respond or agree. With him, things were permeable, harmonious, at rest in knowing.

Several weeks later, the people from the farm called to say that St. Barbe had died in Saskatchewan. He was 93. He had planted and organized and inspired others to plant over 25 billion trees all over the globe. I grieved losing him. He taught me so much with his gentle commitment, strength and love. His life inspired me then and it continues to inspire me now. His life was a blessing.

To get to the story of the other elder who influenced me while I was in my 30s, I have to give you this prelude which took place one sunny spring afternoon at our save the whales office in Bolinas. That day, the genial bluegrass musician Peter Rowan came to visit Joan McIntyre, who headed Project Jonah. I was working at my desk while the two of them chatted. Glancing up, I noticed that the entire back of Rowan's denim jacket was filled with a beautiful hand embroidered red Buddha.

The image magnetized me; I couldn't take my eyes off it. In fact seeing that red Buddha awakened intense feelings, though it would have been hard to describe them in words. Startled by that intensity, I looked away. But I couldn't help gazing at the red Buddha again. And an odd question popped up and repeated itself. Why is the Buddha red? Why is the Buddha red? And why did it seem so important to understand the answer? How strange. After all, it was just an image of a serene red Buddha with rainbow light rays radiating all around it, embroidered on the back of a jacket. Wasn't it?

Red, the color of roses, hibiscus flowers, bougainvillea, lipstick and sunset, is a hot-blooded, passionate hue. Whereas I was under the impression that a Buddha was supposed to be dispassionate and compassionate. Even if he was unorthodox, I really did not want that red Buddha to disappear from my view. He tugged at my heart, fanning the embers of some elusive recollection that still had the power to draw me. My rational mind was pixilated, wondering what all the fuss was about. But my deeper mind was happy, as one is upon seeing a dear old friend again.

The psyche whirls and weaves its apparently artless synchronicities, drawing us deeper into the heart's fields and illuminating the hidden patterns of our lives. Artless synchronicities whose meaning we may contemplate, given the time and space. That's what I'm doing these days. Visible life is like the tip of the iceberg. What moves us comes from far deeper levels and layers, places we do not have access to with our conscious mind, at least not at this stage of our spiritual development. So it was with the first appearance of the red Buddha. For several days after the incident with Peter Rowan's jean jacket, I had a constant companion because I saw the luminous red Buddha sitting in the midst of space wherever I looked. Hmmm. So beautiful, so peaceful. And appearing that way right in the midst of space. It was as if something inside me was saying now you've come this far. You've seen the red Buddha and seeing him has stirred you up. There was a kind of urgency about it. Past karmic connection, the Tibetans would say.

A year after I saw the beautiful red Buddha on the back of Peter Rowan's jacket, Ponderosa Pine took me to a Dharma talk on the Divine Feminine. The outing was his birthday present to me, and it turned out to be a very good gift indeed, one that has stood the test of time. The Divine Feminine was a subject about which I was woefully ignorant. Even though I had lived over three decades and mothered a child I was still tangled up in acting like a guy. Men were the ones who had the power and status, weren't they?

As a little girl, I was convinced that females were superior to males. It seemed obvious that girls were often kinder, wiser and more aware than boys. I couldn't understand why boys were allowed more latitude than girls were or why their cruelty was accepted as something natural. I wondered if boys were given special treatment because people felt sorry for them and wanted to hide the truth about their innate shortcomings from them. But why would people want to do that? The whole thing mystified me. And I felt deeply insulted by it. It made me so mad that I never wanted to wear dresses. I hated playing with dolls. Girls were better than boys, but because girls were humiliated, I didn't want to be like a girl. I didn't want to be taken advantage of. I didn't want to be ignored. And most of all, I wanted to be free to enjoy myself without the restrictions girls faced.

You try harder to reach the same place as the boys, yet you get less recognition and less respect than they do. All you hear about is God the Father, how humanity lost Paradise because of Eve, how women are born to serve and suffer. Then you want to wear the pants and go on the warpath.

You take to wearing the pants, and you know you're on the warpath, but you've lost something along the way. That's what happened to me. During adolescence I was a seeth-ing creature filled with bitter resentments. A girl had to be careful of so many things. I didn't want to attract too much attention, because attention contained implicitly within it the seeds of disapproval and even violation. I had learned that I had to mute myself, even make myself nearly invisible. Fit in. And never forget to be on the watch. I was divided against myself, uneasy about my place in the world. More than anything, I wanted to find a way out of the terrible confinement that was the lot of girls. So I protected myself by acting like a man.

How strange to remember the way I was then. *Nyingje*, as the Tibetans say when they want to express compassion toward another being. They always say that word with a smile and a soft light in their eyes. *Nyingje* to my dear little Blackbird with her long dark hair and graceful body, her anger, confusion and yearning to be free. There she sits on the floor next to her skinny, long-haired, bearded lover Ponderosa Pine, waiting for the Dharma talk to begin.

When I first became interested in Tibetan Buddhism, I had no idea of how important the Divine Feminine was within the tradition. In one Tibetan Buddhist confession, the fault that is admitted is simply that we have left the Mother and become otherwise. According to the teachings, we live and die within radiantly uncontrived and all-pervasive space, the yoni or secret place of the Great Mother. The Tibetans sometimes say that the moment of enlightenment is like recognizing your Mother and jumping back onto her lap.

I had never heard any of that nor had I learned anything about the history of profound women practitioners and teachers that stretch from ancient times in Tibet to the present day. Instead it seemed that all the Tibetan spiritual teachers were men. I was sensitive to the absence of women teachers and I wondered whether Tibetan Buddhism was "just another male-dominated trip" as I described it then. Yet Tibetan Buddhism felt deeply familiar to me. I yearned to connect with a Tibetan Buddhist teacher who was a woman. That longing was not merely something that was simply political in nature. It had its source in the deep sense of confusion and loss that had haunted me from childhood.

That evening, quite a crowd of spiritual seekers was packed together into the living room of the home in Berkeley where the event was being held. The audience was mainly a gaggle of young, white hippies with a sprinkling of psychologists and other professionals. All of us were novices to the rarified business of attending Tibetan Buddhist spiritual teachings because Tibetan teachers had just begun to appear in America. It didn't matter if you had been raised Protestant, Catholic, Jewish or with no particular religion. Tibetan Buddhism, with its elaborate ritual empowerments, mantras, heady philosophical perspectives and intertwined tantric deities, was exotic and psychedelic, a display very much in tune with the times.

We all sat together on the floor. Even if you are young and relatively flexible it's not that comfortable to sit that way when you've sat in chairs all your life. But we had to sit on the floor. It was part of the tradition, a sign of respect. Humbling yourself is a necessary part of becoming a more spiritual person. You had to cross your legs in at least a half lotus position, and you had to sit still. A few of the people in the audience sat that way while we waited. They were very still, their eyes closed, meditating as best they could while the rest of us talked quietly but excitedly.

The atmosphere was filled the kind of ebullience and hope that bubbles up when one goes in quest of grace. Finally the speaker entered the room. Sister Palmo, an Englishwoman who had become a Tibetan Buddhist nun, was a heavyset woman in her early sixties. She wore the traditional maroon robes of the ordained sangha. Her robes and especially her shaved head unsettled me. Oh no. I don't want to have to become a nun, I thought worriedly, as if her religious status might be contagious. As I have mentioned before, I was very protective of my freedom and independence, even though I was also keenly aware that I was neither free nor independent. Such are the desperate contradictions of our condition, which is, let's face it, rather compromised.

Once I dropped the business about her being a nun, I saw that Sister Palmo had beautiful deep-set gray eyes and a very gentle smile. She looked at all of the faces in that full room with a gaze full of tenderness and began to speak about the Enlightened Feminine in a soft, melodious voice.

Several times during her talk, I was startled to see bright rays of white light flash from her eyes. Who knows why or how these things happen? They may have some explanation for rays of light flashing from the eyes in India or Tibet, but I've never heard it discussed in America. What surprised me about it was the contrast between her gentleness and the piercing, powerful quality of the rays that flew from her eyes like arrows. I think they pierced me; I was hooked.

What I remember most about that evening was the feeling of peace that came over me in hearing her teach. Her stillness inspired me. I was moved by her patience and gentle humor. Calm and lovingkindness emanated from her like cool rays. The small hurt child within me breathed a sigh of relief. At last, a holy mother. A safe haven. The truth is, I was terribly parched; she was a beautiful fountain. She embodied everything about the feminine that I had disowned in my efforts to make myself invulnerable.

Though I have no notes from that evening, I'm sure Sister Palmo must have spoken about the qualities of Tara, the female Buddha, and the many forms that she takes, some peaceful, some fierce. She must have talked about the dakinis, those magical enlightened females known as sky dancers. Certainly she spoke of lovingkindness, compassion and the perfection of wisdom. I imagine that she spoke about what it means to enter the spiritual path.

Surely she told us about the four thoughts that turn the mind to Dharma: The preciousness of this human life, the truth of impermanence, the laws of karma and the suffering that permeates cyclic existence. She must have spoken of these things, if not that evening, then in the other teachings she gave during her visit.

I made an appointment to see her a few days after that first talk. Carrying an armful of lilacs as an offering, I bounded out of my car and headed for the front door of the home where she was staying. The sound of the doorbell was beautiful. The sun on the new leaves of the trees was marvelous. The scent of the lilacs was intoxicating. The spring air was fresh and fragrant. I felt blissful, lighter than air.

During our visit she listened to my grave concerns and my spiritual aspirations, gazing at me with those gentle gray eyes and that beautiful smile. It was the first time in my life that I felt completely loved and accepted. Should I say that again? Perhaps not, but it is certainly worthwhile noting the moment, which was as much a way station as the evening when I walked into Lex Hixon's big meditation room and gazed at the photos on the mantle of spiritual masters, exotic beings who seemed so distant and exalted. Now here I was in the presence of a holy mother, and she loved and accepted me. The tangled collection I carried within me began to relax and unwind.

During our interview, Sister Palmo asked, "Have you chosen a teacher?" I explained to her how I had been studying with Tarthang Tulku and attending meditations at Lama Kunga Rinpoche's center. "But have you chosen a teacher?" she asked again. I was stymied. I had never considered the need for that. "You must choose, you know." I'm sure my face must have had a surprised look. Wasn't she my teacher? Of course she was. "I feel as if you are my teacher," I said nervously. "Yes," she replied gently, "but you must consider this matter of examining and choosing a teacher carefully. It is very important. Consider the teacher's qualities. Consider your connection to the teacher. Then choose. It's essential to do this."

Up until the time of that conversation, spiritual teachers seemed to be a phenomena that by some stroke of fortune just appeared magically in my life. I loved going to Lama Kunga Rinpoche's Dharma center high in the hills and meditating in that shrine room where a skyful of stars shone outside the big windows. It was powerful to be with Tarthang Tulku Rinpoche. I had learned a great deal from him. And Sister Palmo herself was a marvelous presence for whom I felt a great deal of love. But my conversation with her that day opened up the subject of my relationship to spiritual teachers in a completely new way. I began to consider the apparently serious matter of how to examine and choose a spiritual guide.

Even if Sister Palmo hadn't been one of my teachers, I would have admired her remarkable dedication to serving others. Born in England, she was educated at Oxford and the Sorbonne. In college, she met and married an aristocratic man from India whose father was the head of the Sikh religion. After their marriage, the couple lived in India where both were followers of Gandhi. After India won its independence, Sister Palmo, then named Freda Bedi, turned her attention to the refugees of the India-Pakistan partition. In 1959, when the Chinese invaded Tibet and thousands of Tibetans fled into India, she was appointed head of the Indian government's Tibetan refugee project.

Her work with Tibetan refugees was the doorway through which she entered the Dharma. It was then that she met the Karmapa, a famous Tibetan master. She said that she knew when she saw him that her life would be changed forever. She recognized immediately that he was her spiritual teacher. By then, her children were grown. She and her husband agreed to change the form of their relationship so that each could follow their spiritual paths more fully. He became a yogi, and she a Tibetan Buddhist nun. The form of their relationship changed dramatically, yet they remained close.

As I attended more of her teachings, I realized that Sister Palmo's devotion to the Karmapa suffused everything she was and did. She placed her life within the embrace of the guru in a way that was difficult for me to imagine. Later, in one of the letters she sent me from Nepal, Sister Palmo said, "Everything happens through the grace of the guru." That phrase provoked me terribly. It was very much at odds with my attitudes and beliefs. How could I submit my hard-earned independence? Why should I? Or was it something completely different from that?

When I slowed down enough to feel my feelings, I knew I wanted to embody more wisdom and joy, to live in a more profound and authentic way, like Sister Palmo and other Tibetan Buddhist teachers I had begun to meet. I felt burdened by my habits and narrow concerns. But I was also quite attached to remaining as I was. "We fear change," as one of the characters in that dippy movie Wayne's World said, his eyes wide and face frozen. I resembled that.

The news went out that Sister Palmo would be offering a Refuge ceremony for those who wanted to commit to following the Buddhist path. I had made an attempt to take Refuge the year before with Kalu Rinpoche, but when I mentioned my intention to Lama Kunga, he looked at me rather fiercely, which was unusual in itself since he was quite a mild person. "Do you know what you're doing?" he asked me forcefully. "Do you know what taking Refuge means?" I looked down because I was uncomfortable. I didn't know. I was daunted by his fierceness. He seemed to be saying that it was a big step, something that required some careful consideration. He was implying I was not taking it seriously enough. So I didn't take Refuge that year with Kalu Rinpoche.

But by the time I met Sister Palmo I thought I understood what it meant to go for Refuge. I recognized that it was not simply participating in a formal ritual in order to become a Buddhist. I understood that it was not simply a matter of receiving a blessing. I realized that taking Refuge would mean shifting my allegiance. The thing is, I already had quite a nice assortment of rickety refuges and I was very faithful to them even though they had not been very satisfactory. It turned out that even when I did get a better job, a better lover, more money or a nicer place to live it didn't bring permanent happiness. Of course all my dreams never had come true simultaneously, I would tell myself. So I never had a real test. But suppose that by some sudden stroke of luck all my dreams did come true all at once and I lived in a marvelous city in a gorgeous house with a fabulously loving partner who was also a great father to my daughter, and I had quite a large bank account and a high paying prestigious job. Even if all that happened, would the satisfaction be meaningful or lasting?

You don't have to be a great wizard or yogi to figure this out. The wealthy and famous seem to have it all, but they still suffer. Nobody wants to suffer, and I am no exception. I was hoping that Refuge would speed up the process. I would have liked instant results, though I suspected to get instant results would be a miracle and it might not occur due to my lousy karma.

The idea of taking Refuge made me more aware of my existential dilemma. From the outside, everything in my world looked fairly ordinary and stable. I was the mother of a young daughter. I was working for a nonprofit whose director looked a bit like a weasel. I contributed articles to several publications. I had friends. I had a lover. But existentially, when the outer gloss was stripped away, I sometimes felt like a person caught in a tremendous storm, blown around like a leaf or some fragile layer of silk dating from whenever it was I began this journey, certainly long before this lifetime and its particular story. Like most human beings, I did my best to hide from this terrifying experience of groundlessness whenever it arose.

In Tibetan the word for Refuge means "to be protected by." I yearned for spiritual protection, a respite from the bombardment and confusion of everyday life. I was afraid of being swallowed up in the murk of worldly existence. The murk, the gloomy darkness. I longed for blessing magic, powerful enlightened allies and friends in the invisible realms. Heaven knows I needed all the help I could get if

I were to shift my allegiance, to stop devoting the beautiful substance of my faith to the attainment of ordinary goals, opening my heart and commitment to a bigger vision.

The notion of waking up and becoming spiritually realized usually seemed as out of reach as traveling to outer space. Even more so. I would think about the large photographs of beautiful spiritual masters that were displayed on the walls of Tarthang Tulku's Nyingma Institute. Those faces were awe-inspiring. I thought of Sister Palmo and the Karmapa. I was far far far from that. The recognition was painful. But the yearning remained.

Did I know then that taking Refuge would not only mean being sheltered by a mantle of spiritual protection, but that it would also mean becoming a refugee? And that the work of becoming a refugee would mean giving up attachment to security and becoming comfortable with groundlessness? No, of course I didn't know it then. The spiritual path is quite a paradox. On the one hand, the mystics tell you there is no traveler, no path, no destination or goal. On the other hand, there is an extraordinary amount of difficult work that absolutely must happen within for any change to occur.

But back to the story of the day Sister Palmo gave the Buddhist vows of Refuge. It was May 13th, a beautiful full moon day in spring. My arms again full of lilacs, I joined a crowded roomful of devotees. I felt very happy. There was no doubt whatsoever in my mind that the Dharma was a divine vehicle and trustworthy path. It was like coming home. The room was resplendent with flowers, fragrant with the scent of incense. Sister Palmo sat on the teacher's throne.

I wish you could have seen our faces. Time suspended, and we sat in brightness. Our tumult was stilled. Nourished and quieted, we looked around like people who had been under a spell for some time, who were just awakening. And so we were. Refuge sank into us, a profound inner sanctuary, a great dharma banner, a mirror. We repeated the Refuge verses three times. "I take Refuge in the Buddha. I take Refuge in the Dharma. I take Refuge in the Sangha. I take Refuge this day until all beings limitless as the sky have attained enlightenment." During the ceremony, Sister Palmo cut a bit of hair from each of our heads, symbolizing our renunciation of ordinary life and our commitment to the spiritual path.

In taking Refuge, I knew I was acknowledging the separation between myself and the enlightened state. I was admitting that even though I innately had the Buddha nature, it was obscured from me. By taking Refuge, I was making a commitment to uncover and purify the negativities that I habitually buried and hid from myself. I was stepping into a sacred circle so that I could practice receiving myself in a new way and learn to experience something precious which I already embodied, but which I had forgotten. I was giving myself the task of recalling myself most fully. And what could be more wonderful than that? Isn't that why we are here?

The red Buddha reappeared in my life that day. First I saw him in a thangka or sacred painting that hung on the wall of the shrine room. Then after the Refuge ceremony, Sister Palmo gave us several empowerments, including one for the red Buddha, Amitabha. She taught us about Phowa, a practice associated with Amitabha and intended for the time of death. In Phowa practice, one merges one's awareness with an Amitabha visualized above one's head in order to be reborn in Amitabha's pure land, a dimension that supports deeper spiritual development.

Five years later, I took part in a Phowa retreat led by Chagdud Rinpoche. Doing the Phowa practice successfully means that the fontanelle at the top of the skull opens a bit or become somewhat soft. Some fluid may come out. A straw can be inserted into the fontanelle. Chagdud Rinpoche tested each of us; every participant displayed the results of the practice. The experience increased my confidence and faith in the power of spiritual practice in general and Phowa practice in particular.

These days the notion of relocating to a celestial realm in order to grow deeper in wisdom is a kind of travel that has great appeal to me. I want to become one with the red Buddha. I pray for the blessing to be reborn in Dewa Chen, the celestial land of Amitabha. Then when and if I appear in this dimension again, I can be of far more benefit. Nihilists and secular humanists who believe that it's all over when the body dies don't give a fig about any of this, but Buddhists want to have an exit strategy, one that brings sacred potential for a fortunate rebirth conducive to spiritual development. The older I get, the more important this is to me.

Sister Palmo returned to her nunnery in Nepal soon after the day of the Refuge ceremony. I missed her terribly. It was difficult without her. Less than two years later she died. Losing her was a deep loss, one that took years to navigate. I had hoped for something different, for years of relationship and learning. But that was not my karma.

I wanted very much to know more about her last days but it was a long time before I heard anything. Finally a kind person gave me a copy of a letter that Sister Palmo's attendant Anila Pama Zangmo had written about Sister Palmo's death.

"The day Holy Mother died was an interesting one," Anila wrote. "We were staying at the Oberoi Hotel in Delhi when quite spontaneously many people came to see Holy Mother, many relatives, her secretary, and others. She insisted that

I get in touch with Bender, her son because she insisted that no other time would do. Much food and tea arrived although we didn't order it. It just arrived and we had a house full of company.

At 6.00 p.m. we took a walk. Afterwards Mommy did much letter writing. At 8.00 p.m. Holy Mother did her meditation. At 10.00 p.m. while I was resting Holy Mother called me and I pretended to snore. Then I told her I was only joking. I said, "Okay what would you like me to do." after closing the curtains Holy Mother gave me many detailed orders about gifts and money to give to special people. Mommy brought out some nice yellow fabric that she put against me. She told me to make a blouse with it and to practice dharma faithfully.

Holy Mother put out her finest and special dharma robes. I said, "Why Mommy?' Holy Mother said, "I will need them tomorrow." She gave me Cho Rinpoche's large picture to deliver to Tilokpur. Holy Mother played a tape of His Holiness, which was advice he had sent from New York. Holy Mother told me that tomorrow I would need to call lamas. I said, "Why?" Holy Mother said, "Yes, you need to. Call lamas, do prayers." Then I slept, with Mommy nearby, a few feet away doing sitting meditation. At one time I heard her make some loud breathing, so I tapped her. She just went. Her face was nice. It was 10.30. I cried."

The account continues, "Holy Mother's body remained in the meditation posture, upright. Her body became smaller. There were rainbows around her. I saw. Many people saw this. For three days Holy Mother remained so.

Ranga Bedi, Kabir Bedi, her children, beautifully meditated with Holy Mother. These children, who had continuously honoured their Mother, provided for her, supported her, now prayed for her at her deathtime. Relatives came, friends came, Indian officials came, in droves they came.

Many people took photos of Holy Mother's body, but none of them turned out. Flowers, incense, khatas, food were offered. Buddhists came from Thailand, Cambodia, Ceylon and Japan to pay their respects. Many Tibetan lamas came and prayed and chanted."

So Anila's letter ended. It's a beautiful description of Sister Palmo's meditative development and her inspiring death.

In one of the letters Sister Palmo sent me she wrote, "In gentleness is all Dharma." That was my koan for years. It frightened me to imagine becoming gentle. I had quite a bit of aversion to it. To be vulnerable was to be powerless, as far as I was concerned. It was only because I trusted Sister Palmo that I continued to contemplate what she had written. There was so much I had to learn about tenderness and lovingkindness, so much I still have to learn. She is the one who set me on that path.

In another letter, she suggested that I consider changing my name from Blackbird to a white or lighter name, and told me that she was giving me one of Tara's names "White Mother of the Seven Wisdom Eyes" as a kind of beacon to help me find direction.

Taking Refuge is something one must do over and over again year after year. It is a pledge to live as a spiritual warrior, discarding piece by piece the armor that covers old wounds, opening the heart not only to loved ones, but also to enemies and those to whom one is indifferent. In taking Refuge, I am trying to awaken from the sleep of self deception and from my beguilement with the outer world in order to join the awakened one who lives inside me.

And that journey began for me in earnest the day I met Sister Palmo. Her example convinced me that it was possible for me to cultivate within myself the qualities she embodied. From her, I learned so much about the kind of woman I want to become. These few recollections of her are not an adequate expression of the positive imprints she made on me. Each spring, when the lilacs bloom, they bring back the memory of that day in May that I first took Refuge. Each time I take Refuge, she sits in the beautiful mandala of my teachers. I treasure her appearance in my life and the ways in which her teachings continue to expand my understanding.

Post Script

"The purpose of poetry is to remind us how difficult it is to remain just one person, for our house is open, there are no keys in the doors, and invisible guests come in and out at will."

---Czeslaw Milosz

So it is not only with poetry, but with life itself.

About the Author

Gaea Yudron is the director of Sage's Play, whose programs celebrate aging as a valuable stage of life. Gaea offers workshops, performances, public talks and individual retirement coaching through Sage's Play. She is the creator, with composer Laura Rich, of *A New Wrinkle*, a paradigm-shifting musical revue on aging. Gaea has been trained in hypnotherapy, rapid eye therapy and other forms of holistic and natural healing, which she incorporates into her work.

A poet and nonfiction writer, Gaea is the co-author of the best-selling book *Growing and Using the Healing Herbs (Gaea Weiss and Shandor Weiss,* Rodale Press, Wing Books) and the chapbook *Words Themselves Are Medicine.*

Her poetry has appeared in *2006 Best American Erotica, Raising Our Voices: An Anthology of Oregon Poets Against the War* and in *For Now, The Little Magazine, East West, North Country Star, Evergreen Review, Provincetown Review, Kuksu* and others. Her poetry book *Carrying a Torch for the Old Flame* was a finalist in the 2006 Frederick Morgan Poetry Competition from Story Line Press.

Her nonfiction writings, mostly centered on nature, spirit and healing, have appeared in books including *The Holistic Health Handbook, The Grassroots Primer, and Yoga for People over 50,* and magazines such as *Berkeley Monthly, New Age, Yoga Journal, San Francisco Chronicle, Sentient Times, Vajradhatu Sun, The Oregonian, Quark4/New American Library* and others.

About Sage's Play

"Elders, by tribal imagination, and by more recent definition, are those who have learned from their own lives, those who have extracted a knowledge of themselves and the world from their own lives. We know that a person can age and still be very infantile. This happens if a person doesn't open and understand the nature of his or her own life and the kind of surprising spirit that inhabits him or her."

--MICHAEL MEADE

At Sage's Play, we recognize that the older years are a rich time of life and an important stage of development, full of opportunities for personal and spiritual growth, social contribution and fresh learning. We celebrate the value of age with programs that promote creativity, inspiration, rejuvenation and inquiry.

We believe that it's time for a more accurate view of aging, one that takes into account increased longevity and health, exciting current research, and the actual lived experience of millions of older adults. Please visit our website at www.sagesplay.com for more information on our programs and worldview.

"Old age is an intensely exciting time of exploration and return, of adventure and spiritual discovery."

--JOSEPH CHILTON PEARCE

Made in the USA
Charleston, SC
25 June 2013